How to get into Oxbridge

A comprehensive guide to succeeding in your application process

Dr Christopher See

KoganPage

LONDON PHILADELPHIA NEW DELHI

First published in Great Britain and the United States in 2012 by Kogan Page Limited
Reprinted 2012, 2014

2nd Floor, 45 Gee Street	1518 Walnut Street, Suite 1100	4737/23 Ansari Road
London EC1V 3RS	Philadelphia PA 19102	Daryaganj
United Kingdom	USA	New Delhi 110002
www.koganpage.com		India

© Christopher See, 2012

The right of Christopher See to be identified as the author of this work has been asserted by him in accordance with the Copyright, Designs and Patents Act 1988.

ISBN   978 0 7494 6327 4
E-ISBN   978 0 7494 6328 1

British Library Cataloguing-in-Publication Data

A CIP record for this book is available from the British Library.

Library of Congress Cataloging-in-Publication Data

See, Christopher.
  How to get into Oxbridge : a comprehensive guide to succeeding in your application process / Christopher See.
    pages cm
  ISBN 978-0-7494-6327-4 – ISBN 978-0-7494-6328-1   1. University of Oxford–Admission.   2. University of Oxford–Guidebooks.   3. University of Cambridge–Admission.   4. University of Cambridge–Guidebooks.
I. Title.
  LF501.C8S44 2011
  378.426'59–dc23

                                                                                            2011045183

Typeset by Graphicraft Limited, Hong Kong
Print production managed by Jellyfish
Printed and bound by CPI Group (UK) Ltd, Croydon, CR0 4YY

Contents

A free downloadable college selector tool can be found on the Kogan Page website. To access, go to www.koganpage.com/editions/how-to-get-into-Oxbridge/9780749463274.

Acknowledgements

I must say a word of thanks to every single one of my Oxbridge tutees; it is an absolute pleasure and privilege to work with some of the finest young minds in the UK and help fuel their enthusiasm for their subject in new ways. The journey to Oxbridge forms a great and rewarding bond between tutor and tutee, and the reason I have so much energy to teach and write, year on year, is the feedback, thanks, exhilaration, highs and lows that come with supporting each and every one of you.

As a doctor by profession, all of my experiences in teaching many different subjects have forced me to stretch my own mind and push my boundaries. Something which I encourage you all to do is read, discuss, watch and learn as much as you can in all the different disciplines. I have been doing this since I first set foot in Cambridge, and I am still learning economic models, classical literature, mathematical proofs and anthropological explanations. It helps my teaching, my social skills and my desire to learn more about our world. If you read only this page of the book, I hope that you will never stop having this same infectious desire to learn which I acquired from my own Oxbridge experience. It is a truly wonderful way to spend your energy and time in your youth and beyond.

To my parents who actively but organically encouraged my Oxbridge application, and kept me going through academically difficult times, I cannot say enough thanks. The way you helped me is the model on which I still base my education today. My sister, Leonie Brantberg, has supported me with a combination of encouragement and fierce competition, which I truly believe has helped both of us to develop. My brother, Nicholas See, is the most thoughtful and selfless person I know, and balances my passion for learning with consideration for others.

I name my Oxbridge colleagues, Sean Lew, Yi Chung Ng (Economics), David Whitehead (History), Voonkait Lai (Engineering), Simon Rees and Chen Yin (Mathematics), as the people who broadened my mind beyond the relative simplicity of medicine, to embrace all other disciplines, opinions and world views. To my supervisors Dr Rob Jones, Professor John Earis and Dr Rhian Lynch, I thank you for giving a young clinician the most incredible teaching opportunities I could imagine, and for professional, as well as academic, leadership. And to my dearest Dr Joy Leung, as Oxbridge is the dream encouraging the students to strive, so you are my dream for which I strive in all things.

Introduction

For aspiring top students, the academic world of Oxbridge remains the ultimate goal. Its international reputation, field-leading research and exceptional teaching make both universities consistently top of the UK's prestigious university rankings. These features are also what make the Oxbridge applications process a hugely competitive journey, and one that is shrouded with a degree of mystery. I have spent many years tutoring students, reviewing countless personal statements, setting essays and practising interviews to help hundreds of students with the application to the very best universities. My goal is to help you stand out at each and every stage of selection to ultimately win your place in the fabled halls of Oxford or Cambridge.

Many of you will already be clear in your minds about the advantages of attending Oxford or Cambridge. For others, take your time to read in Chapter 1 about what makes Oxbridge so different, for both a comprehensive understanding and motivation. Initial preparation for your application with both academic and non-academic considerations is vitally important and covered in Chapter 2.

College selection is often a difficult conundrum, but this is made simple by using the college selector devices in Chapter 3, which also explains the importance of college choice and the roles of the admissions tutors.

I put a strong focus on a long-term and continuous preparation programme. This is because, in my experience, school-aged applicants are very poor actors, and pretending to be interested in or good at something which they are not rings very untrue, in both written and verbal communications. Although I explain several areas of your application which can be improved by technique alone, in order to make the best use of this book you must commit to a sustained organic development of your intellectual potential, which is described in Chapter 4.

The Oxbridge application is about hard work, but it is also about passion and enthusiasm. Chapter 5 guides you on how to take a seed of an interest and develop it down many branches which you might not even have considered in the past, through the extracurricular activities map. It is the love of your subject which is most likely to sustain your efforts when you feel overworked and pushed to your limits. Support from your peers also plays an important role in this stressful time, and is covered in Chapter 6.

The written aspect of your application requires a large amount of time and preparation, and in particular the necessary qualities for your UCAS personal statement are carefully considered in Chapter 7. In order to gain an edge over your competition, you must work intelligently and be ready to prepare in slightly unusual ways, particularly for areas such as teacher references (Chapter 8), submitted written work (Chapter 9) and the crucially important aptitude tests (Chapter 10).

For those of you who have been told that one cannot prepare for an Oxbridge interview, prepare to change your mind entirely, and then work very hard indeed. What to expect and how to prepare are covered in Chapter 11. Sample questions and, more importantly, sample answer frameworks which can be used in multiple situations are detailed in Chapter 12. Fine-tuning of your interview performance, with attention to speech, language and vocabulary, is described in Chapter 13. Details of financial issues, bursaries and scholarships are all addressed in Chapter 14, with particular insight into the college-based funding that is unique to Oxbridge.

Finally, there is a special word to international students, who face an even more competitive environment and some special hurdles, as featured in Chapter 15.

From the moment you pick up this book until you have completed each step of the applications process to the best of your ability, there is a great deal of hard work in store. As your reward lies a place in an internationally renowned academic institution, tuition of the highest quality, a world of opportunities for the future and a truly incomparable university experience. Despite what many people say, there are a huge number of ways to prepare for your application, and I wish you all the very best of luck in taking all those steps towards your own bright new future.

CHAPTER 1

Why Oxbridge?

- The Oxbridge difference
- Advantages
- Disadvantages
- 'Is Oxbridge for me?'
- Oxford or Cambridge?
- Oxbridge selection criteria

I do not need to make any effort to convince you of the value of an Oxbridge education; the reputation speaks for itself. Nevertheless, it is important that you have a comprehensive understanding of the actual advantages of these institutions both to refer to in your application and for motivation. This chapter will help you understand in depth about what you stand to gain from attending one of these top universities. This is particularly vital for excelling at interview stage, by showing admissions tutors that you know exactly why their college and university are number one on your list. However, it is also important that you understand the disadvantages of the courses offered, and there may be some who change their minds based on the information in this chapter. If this is the case, I consider this to have saved you from a great deal of anguish, as not everyone is suited for such a challenging environment, and indeed

Oxbridge may not be ideal for every person. An informed choice will be the wisest choice at this stage, and each candidate should bear this in mind. If you do decide on making an Oxbridge application, you will also need to decide between Oxford and Cambridge, and there are some important differences to bear in mind when coming to this final decision.

The Oxbridge difference

What is the fuss about Oxbridge? When thinking of university applications, parents, schoolteachers and peers will all utter the word 'Oxbridge' to the best and brightest students. There is a special feel about these two universities, and this is due to both their academic and their non-academic benefits. Both Oxford and Cambridge are consistently ranked as the top two institutions in the UK, and very highly in the world stage, often vying with top 'Ivy League' competitors such as Harvard for the absolute top spot. It is vital to understand what makes them so highly ranked, and measures such as teaching, research activity, student–staff ratios, student satisfaction and graduate prospects are important in this.

It is also true to say that preparing for an Oxbridge application is not like that for the remainder of the UK universities. You can only apply to either Oxford or Cambridge, and not both. Furthermore, not all universities will conduct an interview. However, at Oxbridge you can be certain that this will be a critical step in gaining your place. There may be additional written work or tests, depending on your subject of choice. The competition for places is ferocious and you should expect to come up against the top students from other schools.

In short, there is a considerable amount of commitment which is involved in making an Oxbridge application. Prepare yourself for a tremendous journey of developing your critical thinking, verbal and written communication, and depth and breadth of your area of interest. This will, whatever the result, make you a better candidate as a student and future professional or academic in your chosen field.

Advantages

Tutorial system

One of the main attractions for the Oxbridge applicant is the high level of teaching provided. Almost all universities will feature lecture-based learning as part of their programme; in addition to this, they may have classes with tutors, assignments and group study. Both Oxford and Cambridge offer a unique style, which involves a tutorial with only two students per group, taken by a supervisor who is usually an academic member of staff at your college. (These are known as tutorials in Oxford and supervisions in Cambridge.)

As you can imagine, this close level of work is a fantastic opportunity. It facilitates high-level discussion with leaders in the field of your subject. You can explore avenues of interest, as well as clarify important points with tutors who may be your lecturers. You can expect to have as many as one supervision per week in each sub-topic of your subject, as well as lectures and assignments. This is a significant workload, and you will quickly be found out if you have come to a supervision unprepared; there is only one other person there to hide behind! There is no doubt that in the age of rising tuition fees, this represents a very high level of educational provision.

Resources

Access to academic resources is another key feature of Oxbridge. There are usually at least two libraries which you can use, the first of which is your own departmental library, which tends to have a large selection of texts in your specialized field. They tend to be located at or near your faculty, and are also a focal point for student interaction between study sessions.

Your college library is likely to be near to you in terms of location, and therefore conveniently accessible. Although it will have a more limited selection of books within your subject, it does often offer convenient services such as access to past papers and photocopying. The social aspect of these libraries adds a cross-disciplinary flavour to your academic endeavours.

CASE   DM, Trinity College

'Using libraries was also a good way to economize as a student. I found that I often did not have to pay for most of the main reference texts. My college even offers £50 of book grants per year towards the cost of purchases!

'Libraries were surprisingly social areas too. Although it was all diligent study and silence inside, during breaks we would stand around outside and chat about our studies, and let off a little steam. In the summer term, at 3 pm the college would offer coffee and doughnuts outside the library, which was a lovely treat, and the caffeine and sugar fuelled many a hardworking afternoon!'

Finally, there is the large university library, which is accessible to all students from all disciplines, and this represents yet another avenue to explore, particularly in exam times. This is a particularly good place for students from different colleges and subjects to meet up and study together.

All of these are wonderful resources but also areas to spend time studying. An additional bonus is that because students can choose from their college, departmental and university library, the sheer number of different options you have means each one can be less crowded than those of other universities. Many libraries are open until late or even 24 hours a day, to cater for the night owls amongst you. Lastly, although primarily for books, you will find that there are a number of additional resources available at most libraries: electronic access to the latest online journals of research and education, as well as other media, videos, DVDs and many more.

Academic activities

The potential for extra academic activities is one characteristic of Oxbridge which attracts students with explorative and creative minds. The first type of activity will be competitions, which can be as varied as imaginative essay competitions, research proposals, musical and artistic pursuits, or even less subject-specific pursuits such as film review competitions. All of these offer some degree of prize, but more importantly, a chance to pit your wits against some of the best students in your year and earn some all-important recognition for your future CV.

The second main branch of academic activities is collaborative research. This is really where Oxbridge stands out, as the vast amount of cutting-edge research pursuits being undertaken and the number of keen academics are second to none. You can often find yourself discussing a particular topic or subject area, and if you show sufficient keenness, this can start at the very bottom by assisting with the literature review or data collection, and progress right up to co-authorship of important academic papers. The highly active university staff at these institutions make this a real possibility, and in particular you may find your college academics more willing to allow you to participate, giving each student a unique set of prospects.

Apart from such formal activities, one of the wonderful things about the Oxbridge environment is meeting all the fellow students from other disciplines. The collegiate atmosphere really promotes mixing between subjects, and it is a less-advertised but very valuable experience. The network of contacts you can make in such an environment can have long-standing benefits on your future career.

Tradition

The halls of Oxford and Cambridge are steeped in tradition. Some colleges have quaint induction rituals such as running around the courts before the clock strikes 12 times. Even the more modern colleges will have their own spectrum of customs and rituals. You will wear formal robes to the dining hall on special occasions, as well as for 'formal halls' which are silver-service dinners preceded by a Latin reading. If this puts you in mind of a Harry Potter-like experience, you should note that the movies were filmed within an Oxford college dining hall. Although dining like this may seem 'not your thing', it is simply an event where students can get dressed up nicely and let off some steam together, and has a few perks such as being significantly cheaper than dining at restaurants outside college.

Many students, myself included, were put off by the prospect of all this. However, you will find that many of the traditional activities are simply normal forms of entertainment dressed up in a fuzzy black gown. It is a rite of passage like so many other universities have, but also contains within it a touch of class and sophistication, which makes it really very enjoyable.

Extracurricular activities

Most universities offer a full range of student-led activities, and certainly Oxbridge is no different in that regard. Particularly famed are rowing and debating at the Cambridge and Oxford Unions, which also host a large number of notable speakers for talks during the year. Colleges have their own sporting facilities, and often they can be in rather interesting settings; for example, at St John's College Cambridge, you will be playing badminton with full-size portrait paintings of past academics in the background.

For actors and actresses, there is a thriving arts community in the form of well-funded student societies. Students are given the opportunity to write, act, produce and direct, on both stage and screen, and there are large and small-scale projects available to suit your level of ability and commitment. Musicians will particularly enjoy the convenience of college-level bands and music groups, as well as practice facilities. There are, of course, grand-scale university-level orchestras and choirs, but there are also other openings to make yourself heard; these can range from open microphone nights at college bars to performing on the main stage at college May balls.

I can probably say without too much risk of contradiction that whatever interests you may have, you can be fairly certain of finding a group of like-minded people to share them with. I have seen societies ranging from the Cobblewalkers (who enjoy a brisk morning walk barefoot over cobbles) to a gliding society that whisks you away to a nearby country field to take flight in an engineless plane. I should also say to all you prospective students: do not be afraid or ashamed of any of the hobbies that you pursue. What is most important is that you genuinely enjoy what you do, and you will find at university, perhaps more so than schools, a sense of community, tolerance and respect. This principle is carried over to your UCAS application and interview, covered in Chapters 7 and 12.

Subject options

Considerable flexibility is made available for top students, and this is particularly evident in the third year, where you can integrate the study of another subject into your degree in some subjects. There is a huge range of options by which you can take an in-depth look at a particular sub-speciality of your field, often helped by advice from world leaders at the cutting edge of that topic. Looking further afield, History students can embark on pursuits of Literature and Economics, Human Geographers can tackle Psychology, and sciences students, perhaps more than any others, are encouraged to embrace cross-disciplinary areas of study. Some students may be interested in taking a year in Management, which is facilitated by the Judge Institute in Cambridge, and can lead to excellent possibilities upon graduation.

Short term times

Nominally, Oxbridge terms are eight weeks long, although in practice they typically last 10 weeks once you factor in the activities around the start and end of term. This means that you have very long breaks for Christmas, Easter and summer. This is a huge benefit when compared to other universities, as you can take great advantage of your long breaks to get involved with undertakings to further your knowledge and enhance your CV. The university and various student societies offer a range of activities, from charity fundraising events to teaching programmes abroad. Long summer breaks offer the possibility of internships in industry, or summer-school learning in another university, often in subjects that are not your primary focus. The range of possibilities is further extended due to the potential for funding, as described below.

Funding, bursaries, grants

Colleges, departments and the university as a whole have a large number of sizeable funds from wealthy endowments, which are specifically designed to help students pursue worthwhile activities. These can support you in travel overseas, learning new languages, attending conferences, as well as sporting and extracurricular endeavours.

You will become skilled at planning ahead and drafting letters of support for your project. Students have been sent as teachers to China, Japan and Africa, as research assistants to the USA, and on language courses to Europe, funded by the university.

Graduate prospects

The employability of Oxbridge graduates is considered very high by employers, as the extent of intellectual testing and transferable skills gained in the course of your education is valuable. Both universities have very well-connected careers departments, and for interested candidates there are often mentorship programmes with Oxbridge alumni answering your queries and aiding your application. Needless to say, many firms from the City, and all manner of professions, come to give talks and recruitment events, which can be very informative. There are also fairs for careers in the media, arts and humanitarian work. Not only will this be supported by your top-class degree, but these events will also help you with soft skills such as CV writing and interview skills.

For those interested in an academic career, the possibility of research placements in your field is high, and it is not uncommon for students to have work published in a national or international journal before graduation. You will usually be given an opportunity for an in-depth research period, taking the form of a dissertation (essentially a very long essay) or project, which can help direct you towards further study such as a master's degree or even a PhD programme.

Disadvantages

Workload

There is a substantial workload to consider. Essay-writing assignments designed to stretch your mind can be very demanding in terms of research, and you may find you have several to do each week. The short terms mean there is a great deal of information to acquire in just eight weeks, and this can mean significant pressure, particularly if you happen to fall behind due to sickness or other reasons. For some subjects there can be very full timetables involving lectures, supervisions/tutorials and other activities such as laboratory practicals. Even for those without a full-seeming timetable, you will quickly find your time filled with additional reading.

If you find it difficult to cope with the rigours of balancing A levels and extra-curricular activities at school, this problem may become worse at Oxbridge. You will find yourself working amongst an elite crowd, who might represent the top few per cent at school level. There can often be a sense of competitiveness to score highest, and you should be ready to deal with the pressure as well as the volume of work.

Size

Neither Oxford nor Cambridge are big cities by any stretch of the imagination, and you may find that the range of entertainments in particular is not as large as the other metropolitan universities. For those of you who place importance on a bigger city experience as part of your university life, you may wish to consider options in London, Manchester, Birmingham, Edinburgh and the like.

College lifestyle

Provision of college accommodation for three years takes a great deal of the hassle out of student life and allows you to focus on academia; however, the struggles of living with housemates, paying bills and learning what to do when the washing machine floods the kitchen can also be considered part of your university education by some, and some students find the Oxbridge environment a little too sheltered for their taste.

'Is Oxbridge for me?'

You can ask yourself if you like the sound of all the advantages listed above. Do they sound worth the effort of the application process? You should also consider whether the negative points are likely to prove problematic for you as an individual.

In my experience, school students are notoriously bad judges of their academic ability and potential. It is therefore a tremendous waste not to apply to Oxbridge just because you do not think you are likely to get in. Leave that decision up to the admissions tutors. For now, you should try your utmost to gain a place, through hard work as well as intelligent effort. Furthermore, as I will discuss later, the depth and breadth of testing for Oxbridge admissions mean that a few less-than-top grades in examinations should not necessarily be the end of your ambition. One of the most important characteristics is a desire to get into Oxbridge, and a vision of what it means to have an Oxbridge education. The rest of this book deals with how to get there, if this is truly your aim.

Oxford or Cambridge?

There are several key differences which can make your mind up about the choice between these two prestigious institutions.

Traditionally, Oxford has been considered above Cambridge in the arts and humanities, with Cambridge topping the sciences. However, please consider the following points:

- Individual subjects may be ranked higher in the one institution or the other, and it is best to check impartial university ranking systems such as *The Times Good University Guide*, published each year.

- Look at the absolute difference in score and what this difference is based on. There may be small differences in student satisfaction on the course or large differences in graduate prospects, and you may wish to take these details into account when choosing your university.

- Oxford or Cambridge may not be ranked the highest in a given subject compared to other universities, but do bear in mind the additional benefits of an Oxbridge education as listed previously.

- The character of the city and university environment itself may play an important role in where you wish to spend your next three years studying.

- There may be unique subjects which you can study at only one institution, eg Politics, Philosophy and Economics (PPE) at Oxford, and Politics, Psychology and Sociology (PPS) at Cambridge.

Oxbridge geography

Cambridge is often described as being quite nuclear in its arrangement: many of the colleges and activities are focused around the river and the central market square. This produces a lively centre and makes it easy to cross paths with fellow students many times per day. By way of contrast, Oxford has more of a city feel to it, and is slightly more dispersed, with possibly more in the way of shopping, restaurants and entertainments.

I suggest that you take the opportunity to visit both cities for several reasons; as I will discuss later, current students are an invaluable source of 'hidden' information. Visiting the colleges themselves can also give you information as well as inspiration. Take your time to tour the city, visit a few colleges and try to contact students to arrange a brief meeting if possible. One method of doing this can be via school alumni who are now present students – you can ask your school's careers department for the contact details of successful applicants.

Oxbridge selection criteria

In addition to the criteria listed above, there are some fine but important differences in the weighting of selection criteria between Oxford and Cambridge. This may play an additional role in influencing which university you wish to apply for.

It should be said that both universities require high grades at your school-level examinations, both GCSE and AS level, with good predictions at A2. However, the modern era of aptitude tests changes this slightly, as these are tests specifically designed for selecting top students for university admissions. Please read Chapter 10 for further details on what they are and how to excel in these tests.

Oxford has a number of aptitude tests for a substantial proportion of its subjects compared to Cambridge. However, Cambridge asks for specific AS-module marks (UMS marks) in a special additional application form (SAQ).

The result is that if you have a very strong UMS result, this can count positively in your favour, particularly because Cambridge admissions tutors will get to see this on the SAQ. If you have not done so well, however, this can count against you for the same reason. Furthermore, aptitude tests are not the same as A-level examinations, and test your ability rather than how much you know or how well you were taught. Therefore, excelling in these tests may compensate, to a degree, for any adverse AS-level results.

It is a far oversimplification to say that if you do well in your AS-level module marks you should apply to Cambridge, and if not, to Oxford. There are countless examples of successful students who have done the opposite of this. There are also aptitude tests for several subjects such as Law and Medicine for Cambridge. Nevertheless, because of these slight differences in the assessment pathways for these two universities, it is one of a number of considerations for you to bear in mind. The qualities of academic ability and passion for your subject will need to be your strongest points to showcase to either university, and the interview as the final stepping stone is the greatest test of these.

Summary

- Oxbridge education is quite different from that of other universities.

- Tutorials, essays and field-leading expert tuition are amongst the academic perks.

- May balls, dining in halls and extracurricular grants and bursaries are additional features.

- Graduate prospects are usually highly ranked, with additional benefits such as networking.

- Courses may be more academic in nature than at other universities.

- You will be expected to manage a heavy workload and there can be significant stress and pressure.

- Choosing between Oxford and Cambridge should be an informed decision.

- Visit both universities, and read the relevant data before coming to your decision.

CHAPTER 2

Principles of preparation

- Positive decision making
- Academic considerations
- A levels or other school examinations
- Deferred entry

Positive decision making

The burden of making life choices at the young age of 16 or 17 can often be a difficult one, and is being made more essential in the modern university application system. However, throughout this book I will emphasize one take-home message; that well-considered, thoughtful and firm decision making is the cornerstone to an excellent Oxbridge application. This ranges from your choice of subject, university and college to essay topics, areas of special interest and individual interview answers.

Why is the decision making so vital? As we will go on to see in Chapter 7, Oxbridge admissions tutors value not only intellectual potential but also the ability to manifest this potential to its maximum. Key elements of turning potential into reality is making firm choices about our lives and choosing one subject area over another. It is therefore vital to demonstrate your capacity to make thoughtful and measured choices.

Although this seems like a great deal of pressure, I urge you to see each decision as an opportunity for yourself as a young student to consider what is important to you. This process of reflection and careful consideration will ultimately strengthen your choices, and therefore how you come across in both your written application and interview. The following series of decisions demonstrates the series of choices you will have to make:

- decision on subject;

- decision on Oxbridge;

- decision on Oxford vs Cambridge;

- decision on college;

- decisions on preparation;

- decisions on interview answers;

- decision on acceptance!

Decision on subject

The first step in your university application is to decide on your subject of interest. This is a most daunting step and requires careful consideration. For the purposes of this section I will divide candidates into three groups: *specific preference*, *area preference* and *non-specific preference*.

If you already have a subject in mind, you may be classed as a having a *specific preference*. If you have a general direction but no particular subject, you have what is termed an *area preference*. If you have no idea what to do, you have a *non-specific preference*.

For those students with a *specific preference,* this choice seems like a simple one, and one which has already been made. You may well have a burning and undying passion for a subject and feel that it is the right one for you. However, one critical characteristic of all informed decisions is to make sure you have considered the other options. A choice is not a real choice if you have not thought of the other possibilities.

Think about similar subject areas to your original subject. Are there fields which might suit your academic interests more? Also consider careers, future and potential in your subjects and try to envisage what you will be doing in five and 10 years' time with the knowledge and skills you will gain. Is this what you want to do?

Many of you will not have decided specifically by this stage, and you will fall into the *area-preference* group, which may grossly fall into physical sciences, social sciences or arts and humanities. You will undoubtedly be influenced by your choice of A levels; these are usually a good starting point for determining what you enjoy studying. You will have already gone through a process of eliminating some subjects from GCSE which you did not like, and actively choosing those you wished to pursue further. It is a good chance to revisit those decisions and see if there were any options which you overlooked at that time.

It is also vital to consider subject options which were not available for you for higher study. For example, Law, Engineering and Medicine are not usually offered at A level, and less commonly taken subjects at A level such as Anthropology or Land economics should also be considered. Combination subjects such as Politics, Philosophy and Economics may also interest you.

For *non-specific preference* candidates, your task seems the most challenging, but I encourage you that you may find this period of consideration one of the most important, exciting and life-changing experiences in your young life.

First, ask yourself if you want to take a university degree. There are other options which include employment, apprenticeship or practical-skills courses. You may be wondering why I bring this up at all – after all, this is an Oxbridge application guide which presumes you have already expressed a desire for such an education. It is important that you build your application from the ground up, and this means carefully weighing up your own subject choice to make sure it is definitely the right one for you. This will allow you to give that genuine and original presentation of yourself as an individual which will shine through on paper and in interviews. Put simply, you cannot convince admissions tutors of your passion for a subject if you have not already convinced yourself.

As with the other candidate types, you must try to think about your own A levels and indeed GCSE subjects, and think about what you enjoyed as well as what you would like to take forward to a higher level. However, one of the best exercises to do is to find a university subject list, which you can locate on both the Oxford and Cambridge websites. Each one has a summary of what that field of study is about, and is a fantastic resource. The first thing you will notice is the vast array of possibilities; do not limit yourself! Explore the subjects which sound appealing to you, but don't forget to check over those which do not immediately catch your eye; titles can often be deceptive.

The most genuine sign of interest is when you find an interesting subject and feel compelled to explore more and more as your application progresses. Although it is good to take the advice of teachers, peers and parents, try to focus on what really stimulates you, and follow that up with further research.

Subject choice decision-making checklist

Do you enjoy the subject?

Do you do any informal reading or research on it outside the classroom?

Is it something you talk about with friends?

Do you find yourself asking questions in class/after class?

Do you have an understanding of what this subject entails at university?

Do you know what the current developments are in the field?

Have you considered career possibilities with a degree in this subject?

If you find you are doing some or all of these activities, this may be the subject for you.

Now that you have come to the end of this section, I will reveal the catch. You may not have come to a final decision, and you may find it impossible to decide what you want from your future at this time. Do not worry. As long as you have gone through the thinking processes described above, you have taken your first steps towards finding your goal. You need not decide on your entire life today. The beauty of university education is that you will gain many transferable intellectual skills, outside the knowledge that you acquire. A further advantage of an Oxbridge degree is that it is considered particularly intellectually demanding, which is valued highly by employers or further-education institutions. There are Classicists from Oxbridge who have gone into investment banking, Engineering students who have become management consultants and History students who have become film directors. As long as you follow your passions in your subject and strive to your utmost, there are many possibilities for you.

Your further decisions – on whether or not Oxbridge is for you, on which university of the two and which college – will all be considered throughout the book. However, your subject decision is the vital step.

Academic considerations

Admissions tutors often say that they receive a number of applications each year which do not meet the minimum criteria for admissions and are therefore rejected out of hand. It is important that you do not fall into this group, as it would be a waste of one of your university choices, with no chance of success. Carefully read the university prospectus and website to ensure that you meet the specified requirements.

It is important to bear in mind that these are the absolutely minimum requirements, and that you are competing between a number of candidates for a limited number of places, rather than trying to meet a certain standard. The good news is that this means any effort to gain an advantage will not meet a 'ceiling', as you will always improve your chances relative to others. The bad news is that it means your efforts must exceed those of your competitors from the moment you read this book until you have completed your interview.

In academic terms, this lack of ceiling is almost true, as admissions tutors do place significant importance on your school examinations, both GCSEs and A levels, in slightly different ways. GCSEs are commonly seen as a good measure of the general ability of a candidate, and having a good range of capability in a variety of disciplines is advantageous. I am often asked what level of GCSEs would be the minimum I would recommend for an Oxbridge application, and my answer is always the same: there is no minimum other than the specific subject requirements specified by the course, which are often as low as a grade C or above in certain specified subjects. (It is important to check the relevant university website for up-to-date details.) GCSEs must be put in context with other achievements, such as excellent AS levels, A-level predictions and aptitude tests; so candidates with what might be considered mediocre GCSE results still have multiple chances to atone for this. It is important not to get too worked up by the hype of comparing the minutiae of exam results with colleagues – I commonly hear students thinking that the odd extra A* or two will make them favourite to win an Oxbridge place, and years of experience tell me that this is absolutely not the case. However, if you are performing generally poorly compared to your peers on multiple public examinations, this is an indicator that the academically taxing surroundings at Oxbridge may not be ideal for you.

Independent vs state school

At this stage I will touch on a relatively controversial topic which is the divide between independent and state schools. Several admissions tutors whom I have spoken to say they expect slightly less in terms of grades from students from state schools compared to independent schools. They argue that the level of support and education available to students in independent schools may facilitate their higher achievement in the A-level and GCSE systems.

There is some debate as to how this degree of compensation functions, but certainly one tutor said that the most accurate method is when two students have identical grades, but one is from a state background and the other from an independent school; all else being equal, he would favour the state-educated student. This is slightly different from counting lower grades from a state student as being more valuable than a higher grade from an independent-schooled student, as he claims this is more difficult to justify or apply consistently.

Additionally, tutors are quite clear that the standard expected from state and independent school students are the same when it comes to the specialist tests and interview. This is because these tests are specifically designed to rank students in a manner which is not dependent on how well they have been taught.

The bottom line is that if you are from a state school and you have grades which exceed the minimum requirements but do not seem outstanding to you, do not be put off from an Oxbridge application. The special tests and interview are designed to give all students a fair chance to gain a place on merit – but you should be prepared to work very hard for these hurdles as well as to make the required grades.

If you are from an independent school, do not be put off by any concepts of 'state-school bias'. As you can see from the methodology, the main effect of any compensation is for shortlisting, and the special tests and interviews are a chance to compete on fully equal grounds. Statistically you are more likely to gain better grades, but statistics do not necessarily apply to each individual and you must apply yourself to the fullest. It may not be immediately apparent, but as you will see in Chapters 11 and 12, preparing for AS and A levels doubles up as practice for interview; you will need to be very comfortable with the material in your subjects to form the basic structure of many of your answers. Therefore the effort that you put in now cannot be wasted, and yields double results in terms of your application.

A levels or other school examinations

AS level

To students of any background, the following is true: there is no ceiling for the achievement in your school examinations. Tutors have access to your module marks for your AS-level grades, and these are quite useful to them as predictors of performance at university. Tutors will therefore put significant store on looking for the students who have high module marks as well as showing good performance in all modules in all subjects. There may be a significant difference in performance in students who score 95 per cent and above for all modules, compared to another grade A student who is only scoring 81 per cent.

Oxbridge applicants should *never* aim for grades. You must aim for the highest numerical score possible for each and every one of your modules, in order to give yourself a competitive edge compared to others in this 'no-ceiling' environment.

A2 level

In the past, before A levels were split into AS and A2 level, universities were forced to use the predicted grades from a school as part of their academic assessment. In recent times, the access to AS-level grades and individual module marks makes this predicted grade largely redundant. There are some circumstances where a school may predict grades which depart from the AS-level results, for example if the student is seen to have underperformed in their examinations, or conversely if they barely scraped a certain grade. Nevertheless, it was seen as relatively unhelpful by admissions tutors and therefore not of great consequence.

The introduction of the A* grade has injected a new value into the predicted school grades. The requirements of achieving an A* requires both a high performance in AS level as well as a future performance at A2. This means that, once again, the school's assessment of the probability of achieving A* grades is a useful measure to distinguish between a group of very capable students and select the best candidates.

How will this impact you? First, you need to make sure that you are achieving high results. As discussed previously, aiming for grades is not enough, and you must try and look at each module as being an opportunity to score as highly as humanly possible. Second, you must be able to achieve the required offer, which is, for most subjects, A*AA, with the A* subject *not* specified. I impressed upon you that achieving an A* is no mean feat, and you must feel confident in making this set of grades in order to seal your place in Oxbridge, after all the hard work to gain an offer.

Last, and in some ways of equal significance, you must gain predicted grades of the highest order from your school to give you yet another competitive advantage over those who lag behind.

How can you achieve this? There is no shortcut for getting good predicted grades; much like the school reference, this can only be expected if you put in a reciprocal effort. Try to undertake the following activities:

- Hand in assignments and projects on time, and completed to a very high standard.

- Pay particular attention to coursework as this gives an indicator of your performance on future coursework assignments – it should be as flawless as possible.

- Prepare as carefully for internal/mock exams as for your public exams. This shows a consistency of performance which makes it easier to predict you top grades.

- Make life easy for the teacher. Organize your work carefully, write neatly and in large print, and use headings and diagrams where necessary. You are more likely to leave a good impression if your work has excellent content and is also easy to read.

- Avoid arrogance at all costs. Be polite, humble, listen first and ask intelligent and well-thought-out questions. Teachers who dislike you may wish to bring you down a peg, or may think that you overestimate your own ability and may predict you lower grades on that basis.

Remember that there are several areas of your application which are judged by admissions tutors but not written by yourself; these include the teacher reference and predicted grades. Students commonly make the mistake of overlooking these areas, when they can gain a significant advantage over the less-well-prepared student. The most important thing is not to try and 'suck up' or impress the teacher in an artificial way. A consistent, humble and dedicated approach with high performance throughout the year will secure you the genuine support of your teachers, which will come across in their assessments. For further information on the teacher reference, see Chapter 8.

Deferred entry

It is possible to apply for a deferred entry in order to undertake a gap year before commencing. However, the universities and colleges all agree that the only candidates to be accepted for deferred will be the strongest in the groups. This is because you will be competing with not only the students in your year but also the theoretical students in the upcoming year.

KEY POINT

Applying for deferred entry will decrease your chances of success. Only consider this if you are very confident in your entire application.

Gap-year students

For students who are currently on a gap year and applying, the extra difficulty seen by deferred-entry students does not affect your chances. In fact, admissions tutors see several advantages in taking a gap year, including increased maturity and demonstrating an independent nature. Furthermore, your profile of innovation and dedication can be enhanced by some of the activities which you will undertake during your gap year; working and travelling may not seem like very 'productive' pursuits, but they do nevertheless give you valuable experience in a position of responsibility and opportunities to learn about interactions in the workplace. There can be strong benefits to travelling, particularly in social science and arts and humanities subjects, as you will get to see other cultures and their practices first hand, broadening your range and understanding of humanity as a whole.

Therefore, you should not be averse to planning a gap year, particularly if there is a specific activity which you wish to undertake. Try to make it as structured and official as possible – 'a bit of travelling around Europe' will not win over support from any admissions tutors. Some impressive gap-year activities undertaken by students include:

- swimming training at a professional aquatic centre in the USA after high performances;

- teaching English and learning Japanese in Kobe;

- learning Ancient Greek and visiting classical sites of interest in eastern Europe;

- working to fund a European tour with a local improvisational jazz group;

- six months on a methadone distribution bus for drug addicts in Paris, practising French and discussing the background of the addicts to make a journal.

There are really as many options as you can think of activities to do. The key points are to make sure that the activities are feasible, worthwhile to yourself and are planned in advance of your application and interview. Have the names of the specific organizations, cities and dates to hand; this will ensure you can show interviewers your organizational skills and that you have committed to a well-thought-out and enriching plan. Also bear in mind the long summer breaks of Oxbridge terms; you may find it is possible to undertake such activities during your breaks, and this can be a consideration as well.

Summary

- Positive decision making will be a process that occurs throughout your application.

- Careful consideration of your subject choice is vital.

- Academic considerations are the first and most important point in your application.

- Check the minimum entry requirements for each course.

- GCSE and AS-level module marks play a large role in shortlisting for interview.

- Never aim to achieve grades; always aim for the highest numerical score for each module.

- A2-level predictions play a moderate role in selection.

- Only the very best students are accepted for deferred entry; do not undertake this lightly.

- A well-planned gap year does not have any negative impact on your chance of success.

CHAPTER 3

College selection

- College criteria
- College selection algorithms
- Cambridge college selector
- Oxford college selector
- The importance of college admissions tutors

When you envisage yourself at Oxbridge, your college will become your centre of social interactions and home away from home. This chapter details how you can approach the question of colleges, and advises you on how to make the best use of an open day, which is a much undervalued opportunity to actually improve your chances of admission. Finally, the issue of admissions tutors and college supervisors is dealt with at length: what information to look for and how it can aid your efforts to win a place at Oxbridge.

College criteria

Open applications are an option available to you, and these allow you to not select a college, letting the university allocate you to an appropriate one. However, I should say that I discourage all students from taking this easy option simply because you are unsure at this stage. This is not for any statistical reason; in fact, open applications have approximately the same success rate as college-specific applications. It is because college life is very different depending on where you go, and a little careful thought now can greatly enhance both your chances of success and your entire university experience. Furthermore, one important theme running through this book is the importance of positive decision making. Make sure you are demonstrating this at every stage, including college selection: have an opinion!

You should pay some thought to the following areas.

Overall size of college

This can play a huge role in your Oxbridge experience. Large colleges allow you to meet more people from other disciplines and more participants in student events and extracurricular pursuits. However, they are likely to be spread out over larger areas and you may find yourself staying far away from the main hub of activity if you are in a peripheral part of the college. A rule of thumb is that larger colleges tend to have more resources available to students in terms of facilities and funding – this is, however, not always the case. Some larger colleges cannot afford to give grants to the majority of their very sizeable student bodies.

Secondly, there is a social aspect to consider. Some students prefer the cosy atmosphere that a small college provides, where everyone knows everyone. There are some downsides to this: gossip and rumour are far more readily conducted in such environments, and there are simply fewer people around if you happen not to get along with this particular bunch. Larger colleges give you plenty of options in terms of friendship groups and social circles – but this can give you the sense of a fractured society within the college. You can consider this in terms of your own social interactions; is your school's sixth form or college large or small? Are you content to make friends with a sub-section of this group, or would you like the opportunity to get to know everyone a bit better? You may find that you wish to have a different experience from your current one, or choose to remain in the same type of environment.

Subject cohort size

The size of the student group within your subject is in many ways more important than your college's overall size, as these will be the students with whom you interact the most and determine your immediately available support group. Smaller cohorts can form more closely knit groups, whereas within larger ones it can be hard to get to know everyone well. However, more students mean more potential resource sharing and idea generation. Think about whether you study better in smaller or larger groups.

Location

There are practical considerations to be looked at, including proximity to your department. As you can imagine, you will be making countless trips to lectures, practicals and other classes. One of the best ways to plan your locational requirements is to look at the university map, which you can find online, and begin to see the relationship between your college, sporting and social facilities and, most importantly, your faculty. This will allow you to rule out a number of colleges that will not fit your criteria.

The other factor which has an important influence is whether or not your college is peripheral or central. In Cambridge, the relatively nuclear setup means that central colleges will be around the hub of activity: Market Square, with all its shops, restaurants and pubs, as well as the river with access to punting and walking along its delightful length. Being in the periphery may involve a lengthy walk or cycle ride for involvement in social events, and also means you do not enjoy bumping into friendly faces quite as often as your centrally located colleagues. However, the town centre of Cambridge, and indeed that of Oxford, can become very busy, particularly in the summer period with tourists, and this is when those in more remote regions can enjoy the relative calm. Oxford is slightly more spread out than Cambridge, but nevertheless has a very developed centre with popular bookshops, cafés and nightclubs. Very peripheral colleges can involve a fair bit of commute to faculties or social events.

Admissions tutors/supervisors

These can be important for both your academic interests and chances of selection, and the entire last section of this chapter is dedicated to this particular aspect.

Social aspects

There are many other considerations which you may wish to make. Students with particular extracurricular interests may wish to find colleges with, for example, on-site tennis courts or a boathouse. Funding and bursaries are often an issue, and you may wish to research these via the online prospectuses.

Open days

I will be frank about open days: most students waste these invaluable opportunities. There is so much more information to be gained than from simply reading online, and you should follow the rules in order to gain the maximum competitive advantage from your open-day visits.

Prepare in advance

Turning up to an open day without reading up on what you want to see, clarify and discover is a wasted chance. Search through the prospectus and see what you think you might like and dislike about the college. You can almost always find something which is not clear from the prospectus and you will most likely have a few questions to be answered on the day. You can also plan which colleges you want to visit aside from the host college for that particular open day.

People watching

This can be a surprisingly fruitful activity for several reasons. You can see how the students go about their day-to-day college lives. You get to see the variety of people who attend the college and their various quirks. Spending some quality time just wandering about the college can start to reduce your anxiety levels on your interview day by demystifying the process and seeing the people and faces that make up the university. In particular, seeing the academic staff in their routines can make them seem more human and less like a frightening panel of intellectual inquisitors, out to make you feel bad about your knowledge. Take this opportunity to gain an edge over your less-informed competitor and you will feel more comfortable when it comes to answering these seemingly ferocious academics.

Visit lots of colleges

Have a shortlist of colleges which you wish to visit. This will be easier to generate using the college selection algorithms below and allows you to focus on the key targets for your visit. It will not be possible to see all the colleges, and you will benefit most from spending a fair amount of time in each that you visit. Try not to pack your schedule too full, and allow time for moving between sites and asking questions of people. On the evening of your visit, make a note of some of the key differences you noted. What did you like and dislike about certain colleges? Were there any insights given to you by students or the tour itself? What about your 'competitors' who were also on the open day? It can be useful to keep in touch with such students, as another source to collaborate with and share ideas.

Some of my more tenacious students schedule a visit to their chosen college after they have submitted the paper application, which has a number of helpful benefits. First, they take time to find their way around the college, so that there is no confusion or doubt on the day of their interview. Second, they can again talk to students, but this time in a more focused way, and enquire about, for example, the relative personalities of their potential interviewers, as well as general information gleaned from current students' interview experiences. Every candidate remembers how nervous they were on the 'big day' and will usually be happy to give you advice.

Keep your eyes open

There are lots of small things which can be missed if you are not looking out for them. One of these is information on college boards; these are commonly pinboards which have leaflets and flyers pinned to them. You can often find them near the dining hall or porter's lodge, where many students will pass. They usually have notices about funds, scholarships and bursaries, and you can get an idea of the range of financial support on offer from the college. Some colleges include book and sports grants, which can be an advantage. Furthermore, some colleges host competitions which may interest you – these range from essay competitions to the more unusual such as film review contests or calls for poetry submissions.

College selection algorithms

As you will have seen, it is of great advantage to you to spend some time thinking about colleges. The college selection algorithms below are a way to help you with this process; they integrate information from official sources such as league tables and population statistics, and also informal sources such as reputation amongst students and graduates, which is harder to come by.

Do bear in mind that for academic performance, you should refer to the relevant college league tables as this can change year on year; it can be useful to take the average of the past three or four years to gauge the true performance of the college, as the numbers of students are small and this gives rise to some variability of results.

Use the algorithms to help you generate a shortlist – but remember to follow the advice above and follow this up with your own research.

The algorithm uses data from *reputation* – in short, how colleges are perceived in terms of their 'difficulty', particularly by students. How this information has been generated is described in detail below, and it is important you understand its source and why it is so important. Using the algorithm will give you a list of colleges which takes into account your own performance relative to others and gives an approximate idea of the strength of application. Although there will be some variation depending on subject, the shortlist of colleges generated can be a good starting point.

It is important that you look carefully at your shortlist, and go on investigating from this point onwards. Take into account the advice on how to maximize open days. Last, do not close your mind completely to colleges which do not appear on your shortlist. It is possible that a college could suit you that is not generated by the algorithm – you must spend some time thinking outside the box.

In short, the algorithm is designed to help students who do not have a good idea of how to start the difficult task of picking a college but do not want to simply make an open application. Many students will find working with a shortlist helpful, and doing so may give rise to further ideas to help them look for further characteristics. It is time saving and allows you to focus more on winning your place!

Cambridge college selector

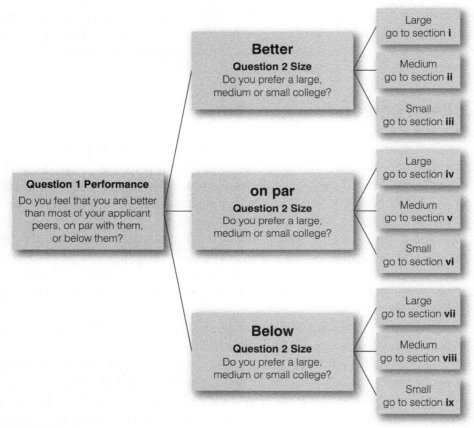

FIGURE 3.1   Cambridge

Section i

Central colleges

Trinity College

Gonville and Caius College

Peripheral colleges

Emmanuel College

Section ii

Central colleges

Christ's College

St Catharine's College

Section iii

Central colleges

Trinity Hall

Peripheral colleges

Magdalene College

Section iv

Central colleges

Jesus College

St John's College

Queen's College

Peripheral colleges

Clare College

Downing College

Section v

Central colleges

King's College

Section vi
Peripheral colleges

Corpus Christi College

Pembroke College

Selwyn College

Section vii
Peripheral colleges

Fitzwilliam College

Homerton College

Churchill College

Section viii
Peripheral colleges

Newnham College

Robinson College

Section ix
Central colleges

Sidney Sussex College

Peripheral colleges

Murray Edwards College

Peterhouse College

Oxford college selector

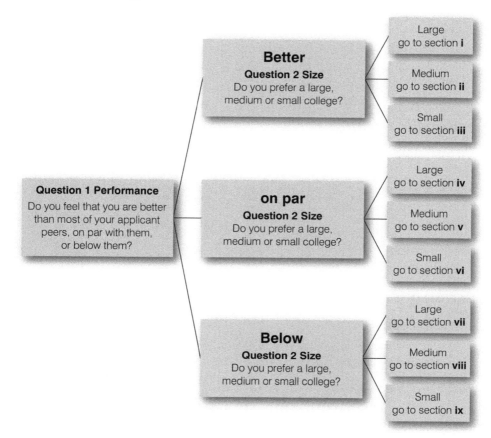

FIGURE 3.2   Oxford

Section i

Central colleges

Balliol College

Christchurch College

Peripheral colleges

Keble College

Magdalen College

St John's College

Section ii

Central colleges

Brasenose College

Jesus College

Section iii

Central colleges

Merton College

Oriel College

Trinity College

Section iv

Central colleges

St Catherine's College

Wadham College

Peripheral colleges

St John's College

Section v

Central colleges

University College

Pembroke College

Hertford College

Peripheral colleges

Somerville College

Section vi

Central colleges

Corpus Christi College

Lincoln College

Section vii

Peripheral colleges

Lady Margaret Hall

New College

St Anne's College

St Hugh's College

Section viii

Central Colleges

St Edmund's Hall

Peripheral colleges

St Hilda's College

St Peter's College

Section ix

Central colleges

Lincoln College

Harris Manchester College

Mansfield College

A free downloadable college selector tool with a full breakdown of colleges can be found on the Kogan Page website. To access, go to: www.koganpage.com/editions/how-to-get-into-Oxbridge/9780749463274

Reputation: where is the data from and why is it so important?

Before I say anything further, I should clarify this section by saying that reputation is a nebulous quality which takes into account the opinions of many people, including potential students. This 'measurement' can seem totally arbitrary, which is why I have not put colleges in a rank order for reputation. Rather, I have named the top one or two in terms of reputation for each algorithm sub-section. I do not mean research reputation necessarily, or even academic performance. This type of reputation is an amalgamation of impressions from undergraduates, postgraduates, employees and employers of Oxbridge graduates, and from schools, parents and applicants as to which names consistently come up as the most desirable, highest-performing or otherwise 'top' colleges. To a scientist such as myself, this may seem to be the least evidence-based tool in this entire book. However, on reflection it has a rather subtle type of usefulness. In particular, this information has been collected over years of tutoring and helping countless applicants in their Oxbridge efforts. Therefore, it is very important to you, a fellow applicant, because it represents how your competitors may be thinking and therefore the flows in competition and college choice. This is why I have included this as one of many college considerations for you.

College selection framework

Use the algorithm to help you narrow down your college choice. Think carefully about your own performance, aims and what you want from your own college.

Once you have generated your college list, your work is far from over! You must look at whether the college offers your subject, as well as the subject cohort size as described earlier.

The importance of college admissions tutors

Yet another dilemma for applicants to Oxbridge is the importance of knowing about the academic staff at their intended college. 'Who should I read up on?' 'Do I need to know who they are?' 'Should I read their research?' 'Can I pick colleges with admissions tutors who may be better suited to my application?' This chapter will deal with these important elements in turn.

Who should you read up on?

There may be a large number of academics in your college for your subject, or a very limited number. In either case, identifying those who are most likely to appear on your panel will give the best result. Important members are shown below.

Director of studies

The director of studies (or DoS) for the college is responsible for all the students in the subject for all years. They will therefore have a vested interest in selecting the best students for their college, as they will ultimately be accountable for their academic performance. This will also aid in the college's league table position and make the cohort more likely to win prizes, awards and go on to undertake research with their department.

Make sure you know who this person is and their broad research interests, as they are likely to appear on your interview panel.

First-year head

The academic head for the first year also has a special interest in student selection as they will be managing your studies when you arrive.

Second-year head

It is important not to ignore other prominent academics who might also play a role in interviewing, such as other heads of years.

Important subject supervisors

Again, in particular look for the supervisors of the subjects taken in your first year. If possible, try to establish from current students who these supervisors are.

Do you need to know who they are?

There are several reasons why reading up on your potential admissions tutors can be helpful. They are as follows.

Decreased anxiety

There are so many variables and unknowns in the interview itself that anything you can do to reduce them will allow your brain to focus more on the task at hand. Knowing the names of your interviewers, what they look like and what they do in broad terms will take away one mystery from the day itself.

Increased interview performance

Both the breadth and depth of testing in Oxbridge interviews are notorious. However, each small advantage you can gain over your fellow applicants will add and may amount to a vote in your favour when it comes to decision making for places. Knowing your potential admissions tutors' areas of interest can give you a clue as to where some of the interview may focus itself. This is because tutors will be most interested in asking you questions relating approximately to their own field to see how you perform in a subject which they teach. You can focus some additional reading and effort on this area, which may yield some added value for you.

If you find that the director of studies is a field-leading researcher in development economics, you may find it helpful to have an understanding of general topics in this area such as Third World debt, the World Bank and fair-trade policies. You might also wish to read up about the state of Third World countries and some case studies such as China, India, South America and sub-Saharan Africa.

If, on the other hand, the DoS is more micro-economics-orientated, you may find that reading about markets, production and game theory can be helpful, and you may even expect to work through some examples of game theory or probability and behaviour situations.

Where can you find this information? Once you have identified the broad topic, try to find the relevant subdivisions of a subject. For example, if your tutor is a biochemist, some online searching should reveal the major divisions of the subject into the carbohydrates, proteins, lipids and nucleic acids. You can then look again at the interests of your tutor, and see in which broad division their interests lie. You should try to read the basic principles of this division, to get a feel for some of the terminology, techniques and vital concepts which underpin our current understanding of the subject. You can look at what are current areas of research, and how your tutor's work fits in with or adds to this.

Arts and Humanities students might similarly read up on the division, keeping an eye out for any current affairs, culture events or key authors from that particular division. Again try to understand the basic elements of the arguments surrounding the topic, and you can use these to synthesize an answer for the specific questions rather than memorizing large chunks. A small, carefully chosen list of quotes, dates or other data to be memorized can be helpful but should not be the focus of your reading.

For all subjects, it can be very helpful to read any textbooks which current students are using, and you may be able to obtain reading lists from school alumni or student contacts you make during open days. In this situation, do not try to memorize or learn fine detail – try to generate an overview of the subject, along with the fundamental principles of your subject.

Overall, tutors want to see how you take your own level of knowledge and apply it to their difficult situation. This section deals with giving you a higher-than-average level of knowledge by allowing you to focus some of your energy on topics which have a higher chance of appearing in your interview. This can give you a competitive edge, especially when applied intelligently (see Chapter 12 for further details).

Should you read their research?

This is more difficult than reading up on the tutors themselves. They are likely to be producing world-leading and cutting-edge research, and it is therefore relatively unlikely that you can fully appreciate it without having studied the subject first. It can be a time-consuming and frustrating experience to read cryptic journals and arguments. Nevertheless, this may vary from subject to subject, and once you have undertaken the principle-based reading as described above, you may be able to gain some benefit from insight into some questions which may occur. Remember, the details are not specifically important, and it is not very impressive to regurgitate a few words or sentences verbatim. It would be impressive to understand the theories, laws and opinions described within.

In particular, you may find textbooks written by admissions tutors more accessible than research articles, as these are aimed at students, albeit at a slightly more advanced level than yourself.

If you are lucky, you may find someone to help you understand the fundamentals of the subject. This might be a teacher, a current undergraduate, a member of a profession in the field, eg lawyer, doctor or engineer. You can ask them to run through some of the key works of the admissions tutors and gain a degree of comprehension that can help you verbalize these concepts in an interview setting – as well as giving small subsidiary benefits such as correct pronunciation!

Can you pick colleges with admissions tutors who are better suited to your application?

I would not recommend you base your decision entirely around the admissions tutors and supervisors, as there are simply so many other factors to take into consideration, as we have seen above. However, you can try to align your own sub-speciality interests with those of supervisors within the college, as this may be useful in your career, particularly when undertaking in-depth research.

Admissions tutor guide conclusions

To some, these techniques may seem like a cynical way to artificially predict your questions and second-guess the interviewers. However, I would advise you to treat this research as part of your mental and academic training for your application. Reading up on leaders in the field will give you an idea of what developments are happening on the cutting edge of your discipline. Breaking down topics into their subdvisions and revising them will help you to gain a structured overview of the whole subject. In-depth reading guided by your research will help you to find and develop specific interests. If you are genuinely enjoying this undertaking, it will be a positive step for your Oxbridge interview.

Summary

- Do not make an open application – have an opinion!

- Think about college size, location and cohort size.

- Facilities for extracurricular activities can play an important role, depending on the individual.

- Use college selector algorithms to generate a shortlist.

- There is still research to do on your shortlist to personalize your selection.

- Plan ahead for college open days to get the maximum benefit.

- Watching people can be very informative; and look for college message boards.

- Research college admissions tutors to decrease anxiety and target *some* of your preparation.

- Use this information to guide you on broad, principle-based reading.

- Textbooks may be helpful and accessible to read but research papers far less so.

CHAPTER 4

Organic development and independent thinking

- Independent thinking
- Positive choice making
- Quantitative relationship
- Extrapolation and speculation
- Organic development

The more astute students may have noticed that the previous chapters have put a great deal of focus on 'ordinary' things. Performing well in exams and getting good predicted grades are all important, but you may think of exceptional candidates as having more than just this.

You are in fact correct. The previous chapters have been building the foundations of a solid application. The criteria we have looked at are necessary, but not sufficient, to gain you a place at Oxbridge. Assuming you have mastered these things, and will continue to put in a great deal of effort, what else is required?

Independent thinking is a vital criterion for admissions tutors, as they are looking for students who will thrive in a cutting-edge academic environment. They will examine how you develop your ideas from what you already know, and apply them to new situations, or see how new ideas can be introduced. This chapter focuses on how to develop this skill in anticipation both of your interviews and of your university career.

Independent thinking

There are several key elements of independent thinking which can be summarized as follows:

- positive choice making;

- quantitative relationship;

- extrapolation and speculation;

- organic development.

We will address each of these in turn.

Positive choice making

This is one of the earliest steps which is characteristic of an independent thinker, and is already an ongoing theme of this book. You must be very clear about what this means. A positive choice involves taking the time and effort to look at a situation and make an informed selection one way or the other. It means that you avoid talking around the topic and actively think about each side, weighing up your choice before coming to a conclusion. You can 'actively choose' to sit on the fence, for example, if you think both sides are equally valid or true in different circumstances. However, you must explain exactly why you hold this opinion, rather than simply stating that you consider both sides equal.

Worked example

In a politics interview, you may be asked about the UK riots in 2011. It may start with a broad question such as 'What do you think were the causes of the riots in August 2011 in the UK?' or it may come up as an example you use, when you refer to one of the duties of a government to maintain law and order. The inter-viewer may then make a statement of their own, eg 'The riots that we saw in the UK in August 2011 reflected the growing dissatisfaction amongst the youth of this country, due to the poor economic conditions and government cuts going on at the time.'

Many students might blindly agree, being faced by a leading academic making a confident assertion. However, it is important that you look at the statement and agree or disagree as it warrants, and that you back this up with a discussion and specific examples. Have an opinion either way, and be ready to defend it with a number of rational arguments. However, be cautious and remember that interviewers are also looking for your ability to learn that it is vitally important that you take on board their comments and criticisms. The interview will reflect a mini-supervision or tutorial, and they want to see how well you are suited to learning and thriving in this type of environment.

Therefore, it is important that you reflect on the interviewer's statement and show that you understand what they are saying and why they are saying it. However, do not feel the need to simply agree or regurgitate their thoughts; try to develop them and go into deeper analysis, as seen in the answer below.

'I agree with you to a degree, and I think it is impossible to ignore the impact of rising unemployment and inflation rates at that time due to financial instability in the USA and Europe. However, I think the riots reflected more than this, and there are several elements which also play a key role. First, there may be elements of the rich–poor divide and culture of materialism which played a role. These events happened in communities and areas which are worse off in socio-economic terms, and it is no surprise that the looting involved high-value goods such as flat-screen TVs, which people may not have been able to afford. Therefore, I agree with your statement but I would argue that the overall wealth of the nation was less important than this divide. There may also be other factors such as poor education, gang culture and what the prime minister called "broken families", by which he was referring to poor parenting. Finally, there was a factor which was relatively new to rioting: the role of social networking technology such as Facebook and BlackBerry Messenger, which were used extensively to organize the riots – although this was a facilitating factor rather than a precipitating one.'

Overall, make your positive decision and defend it as far as intellectual and academic ability allow, but remember to integrate new ideas from your interviewer.

Quantitative relationship

Another area where you can demonstrate your deep understanding is by looking at the quantitative relationship of questions and comments made by interviewers. This shows a level of analysis that goes beyond the comprehension of principles, and looks at whether it can be applied to real-life situations. Ask yourself the following question when you listen to your interviewer: Is the statement correct to *the degree that it is expressed*? For example, is it fair to say that in general one should respect human rights or is it never appropriate to breach the human rights of an individual for the greater good?

You can think about quantitative statements in the following way:

Top tier – 100% true

- always

- certain

- surely

- never

Middle tier – greater than 50% true

- likely

- often

- generally

Bottom tier – less than 50% true

- can be

- on occasion

- sometimes

- maybe

When thinking about statements, think about how they are quantitatively expressed, and whether this is appropriate. Are there any exceptions you can make which contradict the statement?

This is a good way to engage in a discussion in almost any topic with your interviewer. Their statement may be true in most circumstances or broadly true, but the quantitative manner in which they expressed may not be consistent with supporting arguments. If you challenge your interviewer on any inconsistencies, it will demonstrate your ability to analyse the most difficult of problems.

Worked example

'It is never ethical to lie.'

This statement is a great example of one that allows you to demonstrate your knowledge of quantitative relationship. The wording of the statement is *Top tier*, which means the author has 100 per cent certainty of it not being correct.

Remember, as in the independent thinking section, to integrate the views of the interviewer into a cohesive answer. There is usually some degree of truth in their statement. For example:

'I believe it is commonly held by most cultures that lying is an unethical thing to do, and this is supported by many philosophical systems such as deontology, which focuses on the actions of the individual; and therefore whatever the results, using the

methodology of lying is wrong. Many religions also prohibit lying in their texts. However, there are also systems which would claim that lying can be ethical. First, utilitarianists may find themselves in a situation where lying to one person would benefit many people, such as a modern-day Robin Hood scenario: lying to the wealthy to obtain funds for the poor. More complex issues might involve a policeman who was witness to a crime first hand but has not read the rights in full to the prisoner, and therefore the prisoner would be freed by a court on this technicality unless the policeman commits perjury to secure justice and protection for the society that he serves. There are further issues around lying by omission, where you would simply not tell someone rather than tell them an untruth. To illustrate: it may be considered justifiable to lie to someone if it spares them harm or suffering, for example if an elderly person did not want to know a terminal medical diagnosis. Therefore, whilst I agree with your statement in the main, I would disagree with the strength of your assertion based on these examples.'

Extrapolation and speculation

Often, students suffer from 'deer in the headlights' syndrome when faced with a difficult or challenging problem, and this can result in their being completely dumbstruck or saying 'I don't know.'

Extrapolation and speculation form the basis for dealing with problems to which you don't know the actual answer. These involve referring to the knowledge that you already have and synthesizing ways in which it might be relevant. Extrapolation and speculation can be useful for written questions, essays and interviews.

For example, 'How much water is there in a cow?' There is no way you will know the exact quantity, but you can use your existing knowledge that the human body is around 70 per cent water, and state that this is probably about the same for land mammals (extrapolation). You do not know the weight of a cow, but you can guess that it may be in the order of 1,000 kg (speculation). Therefore 70 per cent of 1,000 kg is 700 litres of water.

- Try to avoid making the interviewer work for you. You may be tempted to say 'How big is the cow?' Don't take this route – make your own estimates and justify them.

- Show your working. Write out, or say to the interviewer, why you are making these estimates and where you are extrapolating data from. This gives you the chance to show off your underlying knowledge.

- Try not to use definite terms in these conditions. Rather than saying 'A cow is 70 per cent water,' try saying it is 'approximately 70 per cent water'. This makes your answer harder to criticize as it is academically cautious.

There are many further examples in Chapter 12; look over them to see how successful students have made the best out of their existing knowledge in a high-pressure setting.

Organic development

This concept refers to the development of your own intellectual abilities and capacity in an unforced, non-artificial manner. Many Oxbridge applicants force themselves to undertake activities which they think will be highly regarded by admissions tutors; but this can have the negative effects of making you seem similar to all of your peers whilst simultaneously dulling your own interest in the subject. This section will give you examples of how to develop your interests in a more genuine manner.

Be wary of advice you take

You may find teachers, parents or peers recommending you subjects, books or newspaper clippings which you 'must' read. Try not to let them pigeonhole you into a certain spectrum of activities. Try to follow your interests in what you go on to cover, whilst bearing in mind their advice. It will be useless for you to have read a host of material which does not stimulate and interest you, as you will become increasingly unconvincing at interview when describing your passion for extracurricular reading.

Essential reading

Strictly speaking, there is no fixed reading list for each and every subject. However, just as it is difficult to discuss English literature without having read Austen and Dickens, or physics without knowledge of the contrast between Newtonian and Einsteinian concepts, there will be some 'must know' content for each subject. If in doubt, seek the advice of knowledgeable teachers or current undergraduates on the types of subjects you should be familiar with.

Often, if you search Wikipedia for entries about a book, author or academic, you can find a section concerning criticism or controversy about them lower down in the entry. Although Wikipedia can be a very dubious source of information at times, this particular function can be really quite useful in pointing your reading in the right direction. You can look into the counter-arguments or theories, and develop a well-rounded perspective of the subject area.

Developing your own interests

Dealing with essential reading is not necessarily the same as following your interests, but builds a fundamental platform for you to take your reading further. Do not be afraid to pursue non-traditional or standard topics, and remember that almost any reading that you do has the potential to be useful – as long as you are approaching it from an academic point of view.

For all of your readings, remember to note down the key points and thoughts that you have at that time and keep them in a file. This will become an invaluable resource for interviews in particular, as you will not have the time to revisit your material in great depth once again. For this file, try to keep entries to one paragraph, and focus on the following two things:

Key principles and ideas

This is the more important area to focus on, as it will demonstrate the benefit of wide reading to the interview panel. It will act as a trigger for you to use these resources when the topic arises as part of your interview.

Specific examples

These are vital for communicating to the admissions tutors that you have actually read the material, as well as being useful to draw upon for many types of answers to questions. Make a small list and practise telling them to family and friends, or even working them into everyday conversation. You may find that this activity, more than any other, helps to cement the information and give you the confidence to bring out your reading in interview responses.

As your reading list develops, remember to take a step back if you are going too far down one specialist route. For example, scientists may be interested in reading about the evidence for and against traditional Chinese medicine; however, that is not the only subject in pharmacology and you should make sure you backtrack to the core topics and branch down another subject after a while, eg the chemical structures of everyday 'drugs' such as caffeine and how they work on the body.

For the majority of undergraduate courses, you will be expected to cover all the main subject areas before moving on to a specialist research or dissertation effort in later years. Reflect this in your pre-university pursuits.

Summary

- Independent thinking is the hallmark of a student with Oxbridge potential.

- It is not a case of 'having or not having' it; it can be developed like any other skill.

- Practise applying *positive decision making* in your everyday conversation.

- Be aware of *quantitative relationship* and its importance in arguments.

- If in doubt, start with what you know and go on; this is the basis of *extrapolation and speculation*.

- Organic development is the key to developing a well-balanced portfolio of reading.

CHAPTER 5

Extracurricular activities map

- Academic extracurricular activities
- Non-academic extracurricular activities
- How to develop your interests: the extracurricular activities map

I have discussed the importance of your main academic activities in Chapter 1, and I cannot stress enough how this forms the basis of a solid application both on paper and as the foundation of your interview answers. However, focusing on your A levels alone will not be enough, for several reasons. First, you must demonstrate your desire to reach beyond the normal syllabus and your interest in gaining a deeper and broader understanding of your subject. This can only be achieved by venturing off the beaten track of A levels. Second, you must demonstrate your intellectual capacity to cope with the rigours and workload of an Oxbridge application. If you are at your maximum efforts simply to perform well in your A-level exams, then you may not have enough further 'reserve' to achieve scholastically at a university level. Therefore, you must test yourself and show the examiners that your school examinations, be they A level, IB or other, are insufficient to meet the demands and desires of your intellect.

There are actually two broad categories of extracurricular activities, the academic and the non-academic, and both play an important role in communicating your potential to the admissions tutors. In principle, academic activities are more concerned with showing your interest in the subject and non-academic activities demonstrate your capacity to achieve more than your peer group.

Academic extracurricular activities

Once you have decided on a subject and are performing well in the classroom, it is time to consider which activities you can undertake to gain a deeper or broader understanding. One of the hardest things is simply knowing where to start; below are several suggestions you can use to get going.

The main categories for extracurricular academic activities are:

- reading;
- courses or examinations;
- school clubs and societies;
- external events, eg public lectures, online resources.

Making the most of your additional reading

How to identify interesting areas and pursue them

As you progress in an academic career, you are likely to specialize in a particular area whether it is working in the industry or as an academic. Students often ask if they should have picked a field before their application for their interview to discuss with the admissions tutors.

This is a delicate area which must be approached with caution. On the one hand, having a specialist interest shows your enthusiasm for the subject and your under-standing of this inevitable narrowing of your field of expertise. However, it is also a very early stage to be pigeonholing yourself into one arena and somewhat premature, as you have not undergone any undergraduate education at this stage.

Therefore, I recommend that you try to have a good understanding of the broad subjects which constitute your field of study.

For example, when applying for Engineering, you should have a good under-standing of civil, electrical and mechanical subdivisions. Chemical engineering, in contrast, is slightly different as you already have a relatively specialized subject area; even so, you should be aware of different skills involved in research versus optimiz-ing synthesis.

Economics could be looked at in terms of macro-economics, micro-economics, statistics, politics, statistics and econometrics. There are also other slightly more specialist interests such as development economics and politics. It can therefore be helpful to read up on the fundamentals of these subdivisions, if only to gain a rough idea of what they entail. You can follow up your reading with more in-depth coverage on topics which you particularly enjoy; and in this way you will be able to 'place' your reading within the wider framework of your subject. This may be particularly useful in the interview setting, where you can draw on different areas to answer a question in a certain topic.

For literature students, try to undertake some focused reading outside your main discipline. Could you benefit from contrasting examples from different cultures or time periods? Almost certainly the answer is yes. As you will go on to see in Chapter 12 (interview questions and answers), literature students need to build up a repertoire of reading and examples, as well as being able to analyse, link and compare them. Going outside your field will allow you to demonstrate a great breadth of understanding of general literature, as well as seeing the common principles and techniques.

CASE STUDY

It is not often I refer to myself as the case study, but one habit I picked up from work will be greatly beneficial to all Oxbridge applicants.

When I was younger, I used to be quite frustrated with my ability to communicate in social situations such as parties or dinner gatherings. Working on a hospital ward, I had wonderfully interesting cases of knife wounds, escapee drug addicts and even a manic-depressive who swapped all the number plates of the cars on one street. However, when I was at social events or speaking to friends, it would infuriate me that I could not recall the stories off the top of my head. I'd start a story but forget the funny parts or some details, and would be decidedly unfunny in the end.

However, as a scientist, I decided to do what I do best, which was to experiment. In order to get around this problem, I tried various methods such as writing down my little anecdotes after work (ensuring patient confidentiality, of course), and having a file of my interesting stories to refer to. At first, I was writing down too much, which made the file too long to read and, more important, too boring to tell. Eventually, I boiled each case down to approximately three sentences. This made it easy to remember, and catchy to tell.

This habit is something I encourage all of you to do with your extracurricular academic reading. The more diligent of you will read a number of books and dozens of articles relating to your subject. Like me, you may find it difficult to recall useful or interesting parts of your industrious research. Use a diary to note down the key principles and arguments of a case. Rather than using it, as I did, to tell amusing anecdotes, you will use it as part of your interview repertoire. It will allow you to reference the additional reading you have done, whilst your notes will be short enough to incorporate into another answer.

In addition to summarizing events, I found it helpful to reflect on how the story had affected me and give some indication of what I learned or compare it to other situations. For you, I suggest that you try to do this for each of your summaries: so include a sentence on how this reading has affected you, what you learned, any conflicting or contrasting opinions or other 'value-added' elements. This will allow tutors to see that your reading stimulated further intellectual activity on your part. Furthermore, it encourages and reminds you to actively think about your reading material and how it extends your current knowledge.

Try not to think of additional reading for 'show' or to pad out your UCAS form. Take time to contemplate: well-chosen reading can help your own intellectual development and ability to discuss topics intelligently with academics in the interview setting and beyond.

This will become useful in the following settings. However, it may have additional other uses described in detail below.

Written papers/essays

Having a clear summary of your extracurricular reading will allow you to quickly communicate additional points in your essays. This will allow you to demonstrate your depth and breadth of knowledge and also limit the size of each point so that you can include multiple condensed points into your work.

Peer discussions

As preparation for your interview you may wish to undertake discussions with colleagues and teachers about additional reading. Not only will this be useful preparation, it will also allow you to test the length of your summaries and adjust them accordingly.

THE INs AND OUTs OF OXBRIDGE PREPARATION

Over the years, I've had to dispel a number of myths held by my students and their parents, but this particular one is more of a habit or way of thinking than a myth, so I will spell it out as such. Students must move away from the idea that they can gain a good performance simply from sitting and reading textbooks all day. *Input* of information is absolutely vital, this much is true, and everything we have discussed thus far in terms of additional reading, viewing lectures, etc is aimed at this. However, *output* of information is the truly overlooked area. After all, who amongst your peers has suggested ways to actively go about this? Chapter 13 contains details on the verbal skills and vocabulary development you can undertake. However, finding ways to practise takes a certain mindset and willingness to get things wrong. Moreover, it is more challenging than simple study – it involves a two-way interaction that can be unpredictable, and you do not have time to sit and dwell on an answer you are about to write.

This is why peer discussions can be so valuable – they are the simplest and easiest platform to test out your ideas. Other people who would be helpful include teachers, parents, Oxbridge graduates whom you may know, or really anyone willing to lend an ear and give useful feedback. Try to gauge their responses and you will slowly learn what is and is not an effective way to *output* information.

Additional personal statement

You may refer to your complete list of supplementary reading to choose what to include as part of your UCAS form or, in the case of Cambridge applications, the supplementary application questionnaire (SAQ). You will most likely include them in a more condensed form than your three-sentence summaries – and in particular you may wish to include reflections of what you thought about this reading or how it furthered your interest in the subject. It is important to bear this in mind while drafting your UCAS personal statement; selecting efficiently what you wish to enter in this section early on will free up valuable space for you to add more information or go into further depth in your main personal statement.

Non-academic extracurricular activities

Oxbridge applications are slightly special in that the academic element of a student's ability is placed at the very highest level on the admission team's priority list. However, this does not mean that their extracurricular profile needs to be reduced compared to applicants to other universities. It does mean that in both the UCAS form and the interview there is much less focus on non-academic extracurricular activities because there is so much to fill up with academic achievements.

The first suggestion I have for Oxbridge applicants is to reflect on this structure of the UCAS form, and how the proportion of academic compared to non-academic material must be. This should be an accurate reflection of your priorities as they will occur at university level. There is a significant academic workload and whilst you will find time to try new activities and continue past ones, the majority of students have to limit their spectrum to a few, well-chosen, favourite extracurricular activities.

Therefore, some students choose to select a reduced spectrum of activities to continue in terms of their Oxbridge application, for several reasons. First, for the pragmatic reason of the form itself, there is space available for only a finite number of words and you will not be able to include so many activities within it. Second, this is a practical measure to ensure that you have enough time and energy to spend on the applications process, which is itself highly demanding. Third, it is a learning process by which students come to understand the sacrifices one may have to make in university in order to cope with the academic demands. Last, it allows you more time to achieve higher standards in your chosen hobbies and pursuits.

CASE STUDY   Activity density – tips and pitfalls

In theory, I would encourage students to pick 'high-density' extracurricular activities for their UCAS form. By high density, I mean an activity which is a significant, instantly recognized achievement that can be written in only a few words. A low-density activity would be one that has no measurable outcomes or standards, yet takes many words to describe. Consider the following two activities from two very different students of mine:

Example A: I play the piano and recently received a distinction at Grade 8.

Example B: I enjoy participating in extreme sports such as BMX biking and skateboarding.

The idea of activity density is that the 'ideal' UCAS activity has a very high impact for the amount of words that are used to describe it. Example A has an internationally recognized level of achievement at a high standard which can be expressed in 12 words. Example B, on the other hand, has no measurable standard for comparison, and this student could be a veritable prodigy of the BMX world or simply ride a skateboard once per month. Given the lack of objectivity, it has less intrinsic value than the example A.

However, as useful a tool as activity density may seem, I am in fact very cautious with this, as it may not apply to all students equally. For example, a student had a particular passion for Kurdish traditional knitting and spent hours creating huge and complicated woven displays. There are no certificates, grades, regional or international awards to put down for this that would make it a high-density activity. Nevertheless, I actively encouraged my student to carry on with her wonderful pursuit, which certainly adds depth to her character and went on to become a point of interesting conversation during her interview.

This case study illustrates an important point – do not make large changes to the way you conduct your life simply because of an Oxbridge application. If you do, and you do not get in, you will find that you have wasted some of the best years of your young life undertaking pursuits you dislike just to impress an interview panel. Ironically, this approach may also reduce your chances of success, as I strongly believe that people excel in what they are passionate about, and excellence in academia and non-academic interests will come across in the way that you interview. Last, extra-curricular activities take away from stresses of everyday study and it is important to do things you genuinely enjoy, even if they do not seem as impressive or important as those of other people.

KEY POINTS

- Use your Oxbridge application as a chance to explore new possibilities and cement your efforts in your existing interests.

- Organic, natural pursuits to expand your knowledge and activities will give far better results than artificially taking on activities to try and impress admissions tutors.

There may be some subject-specific modifications to this. For example, medical applicants are expected to have work experience in a hospital setting, as well as voluntary work, such as volunteering in an elderly care home. For Law, you may wish to incorporate some public speaking or debating. The study of languages may well benefit from international travel, work experience abroad or participation in exchange events.

Nevertheless, for most students, building and developing your own genuine interests are the best way. How can you continue to do this while maximizing your chances of success? To answer this most difficult of questions, I have created the extracurricular activities map, which is a unique pathway to opening new doors and ideas for your own interest as well as your UCAS form.

How to develop your interests: the extracurricular activities map

This chapter shows some suggestions about how to further your own extracurricular activities both for personal growth and in order to add strong foundations to your UCAS form.

Throughout this book, I have focused on not doing things for the sake of the UCAS form but rather to follow your own interests. This tool is no different in principle, but demonstrates some of the ways you can take your own interests to a higher level and explore your own abilities whilst having UCAS-form-ready activities even from the most unlikely of personal hobbies. It is intended to give you a platform for starting your own ideas. The extracurricular activities map is more of a rough sketch, a treasure map rather than a Google map. Please feel free to deviate from it whenever you feel it necessary. Nevertheless, it should highlight the potential for developing a seed interest into activities which are fruitful for yourself and excellent for your UCAS form.

Example extracurricular activities map (1)

Interest: Watching films

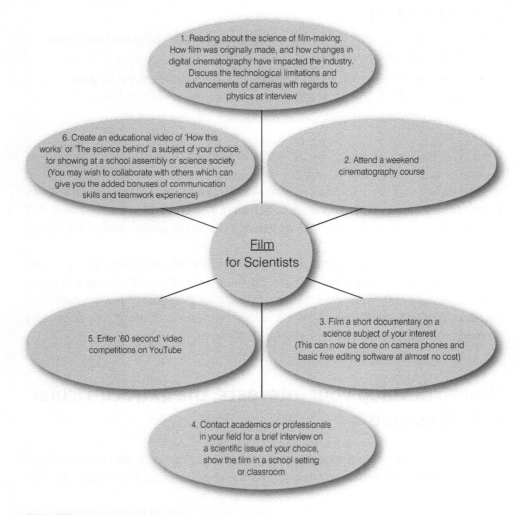

FIGURE 5.1 For Scientists

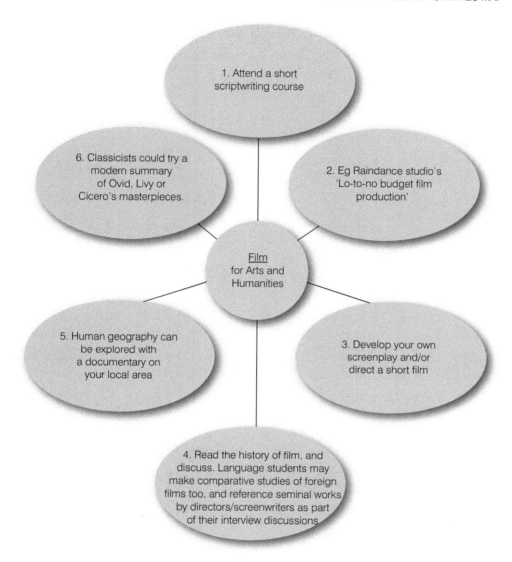

FIGURE 5.2   For Arts and Humanities students

The idea is to take an activity that is not especially quantifiable or impressive, eg '*I like watching films,*' to something which shows far more depth, eg '*I enjoy watching films, and after attending a one-day cinematography course I filmed a short documentary entitled "Theories of the Atom", looking at how our knowledge has changed over time, which was shown in all sixth-form chemistry classes.*'

Interviewers will almost certainly want to enquire about this project, which also gives you something to prepare for at a later stage. It demonstrates your originality of thinking, initiative and commitment to a passion. These qualities are all sought after by admissions tutors and can help you earn a call for interview.

Example extracurricular activities map (2)

Interest: Video games

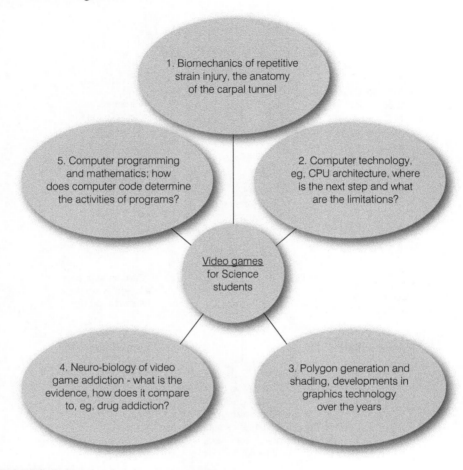

FIGURE 5.3   For Science students

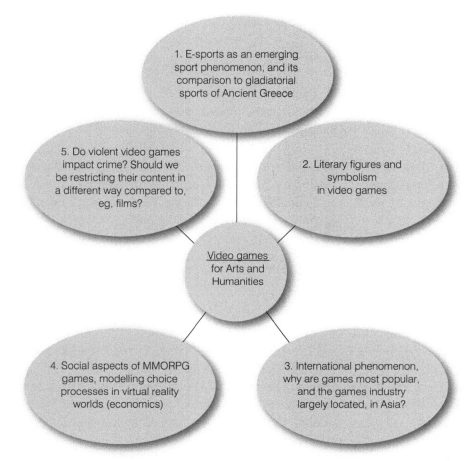

FIGURE 5.4   For Arts and Humanities students

From *'To relax, I play video games such as "World of Warcraft"'* to *'Not only do I enjoy playing video games, but I am also interested in the conflicting evidence base for the role of violent video games in crime, which has led me to read several psychology, economics and medical research papers on the subject.'*

These two extracurricular activities maps (ECAMs) demonstrate how to take a relatively common and unimpressive interest and develop your interest further to gain high value for yourself as well as your application. I encourage you, as Oxbridge applicants, to see the depth of possibilities in any activity. Furthermore, the exploration of the extracurricular map allows you to change passive interests (eg watching, listening) to active processes (eg researching polygon shading, directing a film), allowing you to show your drive and initiative on your UCAS form.

You can see how this might apply to almost any hobby. Interested in dance? Why not look into its socio-cultural origins and write an original essay; or choreograph a show for fundraising? Fancy yourself as a comedian? Why not look at the linguistics and origin of humour or the neuro-biological mechanisms of laughter and its effect on health? Even things as mundane as shopping can be taken to a new level by looking at government monetary policy and inflation or at models of human choice making in economics.

I suggest that you spend some time with your hobbies, creating your own ECAM; you may find the process of brainstorming possibilities a fun activity in itself. Talk to friends and family for further ideas, and keep referring back to your map and updating it.

I developed the ECAM as a system to show my students the additional possibilities in hobbies and interests. I will say to you what I say to all of them: try to stick with those things that you love to do but take them to a higher level. Passion for a subject or interest is one of the key criteria for admissions tutors and it is most sustainable if you have an authentic fascination with your hobby, whatever it may be. Genuine interests stimulate genuine passion, and you should be true to yourself both on paper and in real life.

Spotlight: rowing

Rowing has a particular reputation for requiring dedication and commitment, which in some ways may be unfair compared to other sports, but nevertheless may be helpful under some circumstances. Certainly the early-morning training sessions and the gruelling physical conditioning involved may justify this reputation to a certain degree. If your school offers rowing, you may wish to give it a try and see if you like it; it's not for everyone but certainly admissions tutors recognize the demands it places on students and value it accordingly.

Summary

- Non-academic activities and achievements demonstrate that you can cope with high workloads as well as extra demands.

- Using 'activity density' is a double-edged sword and is something to consider but not to focus on.

- Follow the extracurricular map examples to look at your own interests, whatever they might be, and explore the scientific, historical, cultural and social aspects as appropriate.

- Brainstorming potential ideas can be intellectually rewarding as an activity in itself.

- Refer back to your ECAM regularly to assess progress and further possibilities which may arise.

CHAPTER 6

Oxbridge strategy

- Internal competition
- Peer management
- Family management

Many Oxbridge applicants feel that they are under some degree of pressure to succeed, from themselves, schools, family or peers. They also feel that there is keen competition between fellow students, and this can sometimes be problematic. This chapter tackles how to make the most of these pressures and in particular how to cope with competition.

Internal competition

Many schools have an unwritten rule whereby no two students are allowed to apply to the same college for the same subject. Rumour and hearsay as to why this is includes theories such as 'Colleges will not accept two students for the same subject.' The actual reason may be more statistical: given the limited chances of gaining a place, it is better to avoid competition between two students in case this reduces the school's chances of placing at least one student.

It is vital that you check your school policy at the earliest possible time, as there can be several important consequences. First, plan ahead to avoid any difficulties.

Causing controversy by swapping college choice, late submissions or clashes with other students are all problems you do not need, especially when the teachers involved may also be involved in writing your reference. Try to make the process as easy as possible for those involved.

Second, it makes it more important to make a decision on your college. You must keep an eye out for open days and not miss the opportunities to help confirm your college choice in your own mind. For more information, please see Chapter 3 (College selection).

Managing internal competition between students is another critical part of a well-rounded Oxbridge application strategy and is described below.

Peer management

The Oxbridge application is a long journey and, as with any challenge, you will need support. It can be beneficial to find out who amongst your peer group are considering Oxbridge for the same or a similar subject, and keep in contact about your application. A group of keen students working together and exchanging ideas can have several benefits as well as disadvantages, as listed below.

Advantages

Motivation

This is perhaps the most important thing you can get from your peer group. The collective drive to succeed, as well as some friendly competition, may help you to get the best from your application, and really kick-start your progress.

Resources

Your group may be able to share articles, books and websites in order to reduce the amount of time spent searching. You can undertake shared learning exercises where each member reads an article, book or chapter and gives a brief presentation or overview to the others. This will allow you to cover a greater breadth of material than you will be able to manage yourself.

Support

The stress and pressures of the application can get the better of many students, and a group of peers can be a good forum to vent any frustrations and aid in coping with the entire process.

Economies of scale

Teachers may have difficulty finding time to spend on additional support for each potential Oxbridge applicant, no matter how good their intentions. Therefore, having a group of keen applicants can allow teachers to address a larger audience, reducing the hassle for them and making it more likely for them to help you. This can be in the form of a small after-school talk, going through more advanced subject material or even listening to short presentations on extracurricular reading you have done to check your understanding.

Disadvantages

Logistics

One of the major problems with the Oxbridge application is the time pressure under which all students find themselves. Although peer groups can be immensely useful as described above, you may find the day-to-day organization time consuming and stressful, which can negate the useful effects. If this is affecting you, try the following strategies:

- Ask others to pitch in and help with the running of the group to share the burden.

- E-mail or other social networking websites such as Facebook or Twitter have the potential to help in organizing ad hoc events or sharing information.

Rivalries

Occasionally, the top students within a school will have a friendly or unfriendly rivalry with one another. Since these will also often be the Oxbridge applicants, you may find yourself crossing paths with an arch-enemy (to be a tad melodramatic). You may find that you disagree with people in the group, or just don't click; don't force yourself to get along if you cannot, and be wary of using too much time trying to repair this social problem. Try the following strategies:

- Remember that you will not be in direct competition with each other, and there is far more competition from outside your school. Therefore, statistically it makes far more sense to band together as a team within your school rather than wasting time and effort on internal rivalries.

- Try to control the numbers of your study group. If your group contains a few core friendly members, you are less likely to suffer the ill effects of rivalries.

Misinformation

Occasionally, students who are teaching or explaining concepts to each other can get the facts, principles or sentiments wrong. This can result in spreading of incorrect ideas that may later be problematic in interview or in your written work. There are several ways to counteract this: first, see if you can find a teacher who is willing to help you run through some interesting topics (although teachers are by no means flawless, they are more likely to have a deeper understanding); second, make sure to check any fundamental arguments or facts which you are told about just to ensure they are correct. If in doubt, ask the presenter about their source and assess its reliability.

OXBRIDGE PREPARATION GROUP TIPS

It can be helpful to have a mix of subjects amongst your group. You may find that students who are applying for other disciplines add valuable insight and opinions. Economics, Politics and History students may find some areas of crossover, and mathematicians and physicists likewise.

Sharing notes:

- Keep the group informal. If you run it as a strict club or society, there is more potential for problems to arise between people. This kind of activity is suited for breaks, lunches, free periods and after school.

- Weekend events can also be helpful but do not become frustrated if not everyone wishes to turn up for these.

Family management

Another important element of your Oxbridge application will be input and support from your family. Parents often play a vital and overlooked role, as well as being a common source of additional pressure for already overworked students. The following strategies come from years of experience of negotiating parental policies on behalf of my students, in order to maximize their chances of Oxbridge success.

Parent–student meetings

One of the first problems which students describe to me is that their parents can become over-involved in their application. Students often feel that they are quizzed too frequently about how their application is going or what they are doing to improve their chances. This regular interrogation can have a negative impact on the students' psychological welfare and motivation, and can make for a tense home environment.

On the other hand, parents of students often tell me that they feel uninformed about their son's or daughter's activities, how they are doing and coping, and feel frustrated at the lack of information. This almost always stems from a well-meaning concern for the success of the student and their future and can be exasperating for the parents, who can feel as if they are not being allowed to help as much as they could.

As the independent third party, I negotiate 'Oxbridge meetings' for almost all of my students. The idea of this is to set aside specific times during the week for the student and parent to discuss application issues, ideas and logistics, in order to keep the parents 'in the loop', whilst allowing the student to know when the discussion is coming rather than their living in fear of a constant 'pop quiz'. It is also a good forum to discuss concerns and coping mechanisms.

I can say with great statistical accuracy that 100 per cent of my tutees and their families have praised this systematic approach. They say that it is effective in reducing household tensions, stress on the student and anxiety on the parents. It is a relatively flexible system, as meetings can be held as often or infrequently as agreed by both parties, and, of course, discussions will be brought up as new information or results become available, or as issues arise. Nevertheless, with the basic rules and framework for discussion present, students have universally found their productivity *and quality of rest in the home* increase as their discussions are focused in the Oxbridge meetings rather than all the time.

For any parents reading this book, this is probably the most important, well-proven step you can take in helping your child's welfare and sustainable application effort. Please discuss with your son or daughter how they can benefit from your input and also what information you would like on their progress, and set up some kind of formal meeting to discuss this, which can be over dinner, after school, on a weekend, by e-mail or whichever method suits you. I am certain you will all reap considerable benefits from adding a little extra structure during this busy period.

Extracurricular activities

In my experience, the second major area of conflict is the balance between extracurricular activities and 'rest-and-relaxation' (R&R) activities. My students report that they are often well supported in traditional, quantifiable extracurricular activities such as sports, orchestras or school clubs, but sometimes come into conflict with parents when it comes to R&R types of activity such as going to the cinema, meeting friends or simply 'going out'.

The Oxbridge application does not simply require a high level of work and commitment to both academic and extracurricular activities; it demands this. However, because of this, Oxbridge applicants are generally subject to more stress and anxiety than other students, and it is important to be able to relax in a reasonable framework, in a method of their choosing. Although there is no formal system for this aspect of the student's life (unlike the Oxbridge meetings above), I have had to negotiate some 'downtime' or protected R&R time for students who are suffering from the ill effects of pressure, as they feel they are being scrutinized or pressurized during this time at home.

This problem may well not apply to your family environment, and this is of course excellent for increasing your chances of sustainable and long-term hard work. If you are having problems with being allowed enough free time to have high-quality R&R, please bring this up with your parents as soon as possible and discuss the issues you are having; you may find that the interventions or disapprovals are unintended or a result of miscommunication. You may need to negotiate some framework for your time off so that both parties know when you are having such a period, and will try to encourage you to enjoy this activity as much as possible to take your mind off the Herculean task of the Oxbridge application. As I find myself saying to both parties on a regular basis, a degree of flexibility goes a long way in helping both student and parents.

Summary

- Find out about internal competition rules for college selection within your school as early as possible.

- When managing peers, remember that your competition with outside candidates *far* outweighs internal competition.

- Peer study and support groups have several distinct advantages.

- Beware of their disadvantages, however, and feel free to be flexible if things are not working out.

- Consider setting up formal 'Oxbridge meetings' in the home to increase information flow and decrease stress.

- Protected R&R time for students is an underestimated but vital area for success.

CHAPTER 7

Optimizing your UCAS form for Oxbridge

- Characteristics sought by admissions tutors
- Genuine interest in the subject
- Unsatisfied intellectual curiosity
- Commitment
- Potential
- Initiative
- Academic ability
- How to put these together: creating your personal statement
- Sample personal statements and their structures

The UCAS personal statement is your vehicle to express why you above all others deserve a place at Oxbridge. It requires meticulous preparation and multiple revisions to achieve a well-rounded, genuinely enthusiastic and comprehensive account of yourself. This chapter details the characteristics sought by admissions tutors, and describes how to assemble these together in a coherent and original personal statement.

Characteristics sought by admissions tutors

As with most stages of your application, it is vital to remember your audience. Oxbridge admissions tutors are looking for 'the brightest and the best' students, but this can be further broken down to a number of key characteristics possessed by such candidates:

- genuine interest in the subject;
- unsatisfied intellectual curiosity;
- commitment;
- potential;
- initiative;
- academic ability.

These are the characteristics which you will need to communicate in your written application, to warrant further investigation at interview.

Genuine interest in the subject

The very best academics undertake their research and teaching not because they have to but because they love the subject. Admissions tutors are most certainly amongst this group and in order to impress them, your passion for the subject needs to come out.

A common mistake is to overdo your declarations of enthusiasm without adequate support – for example: 'I am utterly fascinated by the study of archaeology.' Try to give examples of what it is about archaeology that you like; perhaps it is a particular era which interests you, or perhaps it was a trip to Egypt which first sparked your curiosity. Furthermore, try to be economical with your descriptions: 'I am fascinated' will suffice to convey your feelings whilst not sounding overly dramatic, as well as saving you valuable characters in which to describe your other achievements.

Look at the sample statements later in this chapter and notice how the students use these techniques to express their genuine interest in a balanced, evidence-based manner. You can refer to the 'Specificity rule' in Chapter 12, which deals with giving examples in interview questions; this too applies to the personal statement, and a truly interested individual should always be able to describe exactly what causes their keenness and why.

Unsatisfied intellectual curiosity

There are some students for whom school-level learning represents the peak of their achievement or the ceiling of their interest; they may do well in school and examinations but will not go on to achieve highly in a university setting. Therefore, it is important to show that this is not the case for you, particularly in the *academic* arena.

How can you demonstrate this? First, it is important to touch on your A-level subjects as your reference point, and indeed to discuss the points of interest that have emerged from this. However, to truly demonstrate your unsatisfied curiosity, you must show the admissions tutors what you have done to go beyond the classroom. Make this link between A levels, interests and your reading and activities in order to show your desire for more than you are currently obtaining from pre-university education.

Throughout this book I refer to GCSE, AS and A level as the standard examinations which students will undertake or have undertaken; however, I am aware that many of you will do or have done different examinations, such as Scottish Highers, International Baccalaureate, Irish Leaving Certificate or many other systems. The principles that I describe in the book will be similar, and the examination profiles that you undertake at 16, 17 and 18 years of age will encompass these same principles. However, this particular section of the book is the one area where there is a significant difference, and that is because there is usually a larger number of subjects undertaken in non-A-level systems. This can be an advantage because you will have a broader range of topics to link to your future subject of study, and also a broader skill set. However, it can mean it is time and space consuming to describe all of these subjects in your personal statement. Therefore, in a departure from my advice to A-level students, I suggest that you focus on the most relevant subjects *which will give you an advantage* in your application. This does not mean subjects which are all similarly linked; as you will see below, often describing a mix of arts and sciences can be helpful in displaying your varied skill set. However, be careful about droning on about each subject at length; this can become unhelpful and even dull for the admissions tutor.

Commitment

Admissions tutors are more interested in students who have had a long-term interest in their subject, because they are more likely to be stable and determined to pursue it. As it is not just a passing fancy, they will stick with the subject to make positive contributions at an undergraduate level and beyond.

In terms of the UCAS form, you can demonstrate this by showcasing the development of your interest over time: where it started, how it progressed and, if appropriate, where it is heading. You will see how to formally convert this into a UCAS personal statement in the examples below, particularly when following structure 2.

Potential

The Oxbridge environment should get the best out of you as an academic individual, and admissions tutors want to see that schoolwork has not pushed you to your limits. This is best demonstrated by a range of achievements in both the academic and extracurricular arenas. In terms of your UCAS form, your grades and teacher report will form one part of this, but must be coupled with a strong profile of non-academic achievements in order to show the range of your capabilities. Use the extracurricular activities map in Chapter 5 to develop your repertoire further.

As you will see from the sample structures below, this section usually comes towards the end of personal statements. This is because, although it is important, the purely academic sections take a greater priority than this particular characteristic. Nevertheless, it is a vital part of your application, and I recommend that around 25 per cent of your UCAS statement characters should be allocated to this topic.

Many students feel that a large and impressive extracurricular activities spectrum can compensate for less-good academic results. Although I have described in Chapter 1 that there are methods to overcome poor results, such as high performance in aptitude tests, I should emphasize that extracurricular activities are *not* one of them. This is because admissions tutors see these activities as being exactly as described: *extra* to your curriculum. Therefore, a poorly performing student who is otherwise engaged might show that they cannot cope with having such a high demand on their time; and perhaps if they undertook fewer activities their academic performance would increase. However, it is clear that this student has not prioritized their timetable for academia, and that is what Oxbridge tutors are looking for.

Therefore, build your extracurricular activities on top of academic success. If you find you are spreading yourself too thinly, go back to the main focus of being a student: which is study. If you are doing well, you can add extra activities for your personal development and also to show your ability to cope. For Oxbridge, which is perhaps different from your other university applications, you will need to emphasize through your achievements that you are not yet at your limits!

Initiative

In academia and research, the natural sequence of events is to have a thorough understanding of your field before going on to pioneer new theories and research. Therefore, having covered the basis of your background knowledge and reading, this is the opportune area to demonstrate *initiative* within your statement. This will include any activities which you have started on the basis of your subject choice, any pioneering works, societies or projects which may have resulted or any reading areas which are perhaps non-traditional and outside the scope of the main topic lists of your field.

Some students have launched societies, tabled debating motions on their topics of interest, filmed short documentaries in their local area, participated in language courses over summer or any number of activities which require you to go out and do something different. Other opportunities include the Young Enterprise scheme, which gives you the flexibility to be very innovative with creating a product or brand and showing your originality to admissions tutors.

Academic ability

This is the most difficult to work into your personal statement, and in fact although it is a characteristic that is most highly sought after, most of the information on this particular topic will be covered by your GCSE and AS-level results, A2-level predictions and teacher reference (which is covered in great depth in the next chapter). However, I mention it in this section because there are some specific achievements which you may have managed that can further support this. In particular, items such as awards, scholarships, prizes, top placement in academic-based competitions such as Olympiads and similar events. Please discuss this with your teacher to see what they will or will not include in their confidential reference. Last, please note that I use the term 'achievement' rather than 'activity' in this section; this is because it is hard to show your ability by simply participating in something, and usually it requires a degree of measurable success. Although there can be cases where the activity itself is an achievement, this is relatively rare, but bear in mind that many students will have their academic ability demonstrated through grades and teacher reference alone.

How to put these together: creating your personal statement

This chapter describes two different structures; one is more interest focused and the other is based around the development of your interest. However, both have some key similarities:

1 Address the characteristics listed above for the best chance of success.

2 The proportion of academic to non-academic material is usually around 75 to 25 per cent.

3 Never, ever lie on your personal statement. This will be easily exposed by experienced admissions tutors and will be disastrous at the interview stage.

4 Avoid arrogance; the specific methods are discussed in the example personal statements below.

5 Do not make your statement a pure list of books and courses; always include a statement about why you found the area interesting, what you learned or how it relates to your field of study.

Experiment with both structures 1 and 2, and see which suits your particular combination of school interests and extracurricular academic interests. You may find that one flows better than the other, and if in doubt, try to gain plenty of feedback to aid your decision. You may find not only that teachers, peers and parents are helpful but also that Oxbridge graduates or applications tutors who may not be in your discipline can still add valuable comments to improve your chances of success.

Both structures 1 and 2 form two main body paragraphs of your personal statement, which deal primarily with the characteristics of interest and intellectual curiosity. Remember to try to think about any *prospective* statements you can make, eg what it is about the university course that you are looking forward to.

Sample personal statements and their structures

Structure 1 – interest-focused structure

Admissions tutors will know about the limited range of subjects in the school syllabus, and discussing these at first can sometimes lead to rather predictable formats. In the vast majority of cases, therefore, some students like to open with the more interesting things they have done. They might refer to a particular author, scientist or event and discuss some of the controversy or developments surrounding these, as we will see in the following examples.

They will highlight their specific interests in the field of study first, before later referencing it to their schoolwork. This is the mirror image of structure 1. The advantage of this approach of having a 'front-loaded' answer is that it gets straight to topics of a high intellectual level and attracts the interest of admissions tutors. The disadvantage is the disruption to the structure and flow of how your statement reads, as you will have to return to more mundane topics after your 'interesting' opener.

Example 1 – Physiology (Oxford)

Drawn by its intriguing title, I read a book called The Man who Mistook his Wife for a Hat *by Oliver Sacks. I not only enjoyed looking into the range of unusual neurological disorders but also into how the patients coped with and gained skills from their disabilities. In particular, Witty Ticcy Ray, a man suffering from severe Tourette's syndrome, had bursts of wild musical creativity from his tics, and went on to become a successful jazz drummer. I found this book very interesting because Dr Sacks presented the patients rather than just the disorders, and showed the aspects of the illnesses that are not usually taught academically.*

When I first read the personal statement of this student, she simply wrote about reading this particular book without giving any further information or reflection; in essence she was breaking the Specificity rule. However, when I quizzed her further, she could remember some of the stories and cases quite well, and her enthusiasm was also very apparent. This led on to a new opening paragraph, where she backs up her statement of *genuine interest* with supporting examples, and links it back to what she enjoyed, which makes for an eye-catching structure-1 opening. Compare this to the next example, which has less reflection but stronger linking to the development of the student's interest. Both students were successful in gaining an Oxbridge place, and it gives you an idea of the flexibility in your opening paragraph which you can use to individualize your entire application.

It is not only the complexity of the mind that intrigues me, but also the complexity of the human body. I am fascinated by the way each cell has a specific role and how they are constantly working together to allow the body to function as a whole organism. There are always new things to discover about the human body, and I would like to study physiology in order to increase my understanding of it. While studying the AS Biology course, the topic which I found the most stimulating was the study of the heart. I read the relevant chapter of Guyton and Hall's Medical Physiology *and I realized that while we were only taught that the coordination of contraction is regulated by the sinoatrial node, heart muscle actually has its own intrinsic contractility at a lower rate.*

This paragraph neatly encapsulates the characteristic of *unsatisfied intellectual curiosity* by building on school-level work and taking it further in terms of independent study. The student shows an intelligently planned strategy by choosing a book used by first-year physiology students, and furthermore by highlighting some key differences of understanding between university and school. You may wish to look ahead to key textbooks on your course to gain some insight as to what you will be learning and how it compares to your own level of knowledge.

Beyond the school science syllabus, I have an interest in learning about the brain, which led me to choose the topic of Alzheimer's disease for a presentation in class. It frustrates me that there is no known cause of or cure for this condition, but this makes me more determined to explore a deeper understanding of the subject in the hope that one day these questions will be answered.

In chemistry, I particularly enjoy finding solutions to problems by using both logic and observations from experiments. Studying Maths has also allowed me to be comfortable with working with numbers and processing statistics and data. On top of this, I take pleasure in learning other languages and I find French a refreshing contrast to Cantonese, which I speak fluently.

The student goes on to demonstrate how her A-level subjects give her skills and develop her interest, which will go on to help her in her future studies. One theme running throughout her statement is never to make an unsubstantiated declaration: she always backs this up with evidence, links or reflection. This approach is particularly good for scientists who want to show their understanding of the scientific method; however, arts and humanities students such as historians and philosophers will likewise appreciate the importance of this approach in their work.

On a weekly basis I visit a lady who is partially blind, as part of the 60+ reading scheme. In these sessions, I help her with reading and other tasks that she would otherwise find difficult. This scheme has taught me how to communicate with adults and to forge links with the local community. I feel I have a greater understanding of the frustrations that the elderly can sometimes experience when they can no longer perform tasks with the same ease as before. Being a member of the school orchestra and choir has given me an insight into the importance of commitment and teamwork in a musical context. I also enjoy dance and swimming. Trying to balance my extracurricular activities and school work is demanding, but it has taught me valuable time-management skills. For my Duke of Edinburgh's Gold Award, I participated as both a team member, in the group route planning, and also as group leader for a day, which involved navigating to the proposed destination. Participating in this programme has helped me to develop my stamina and communication skills under pressure.

The range of extracurricular activities is broad, and the student has taken time to show what she has learned from each task. You can contrast this to the 'high-density' approach shown in example 2 below; you may find that one or the other is more valuable to your own individual portfolio of achievements and activities.

Example 2 – Classics (Cambridge)

'Draco dormiens nunquam titillandus', the motto of Harry Potter's Wizarding Academy, initially sparked my interest and curiosity in Latin. What I did not envisage at the time was the wealth of knowledge that I had yet to discover in Classics. After this brief dalliance with Latin when I was in Year 6, I was excited about studying this unique, traditional and fundamental language; the paucity of Latin spoken in the world created a mysterious element and an ambiguity about the language which rendered it both challenging and thrilling for me to discover. When I encounter a Latin text, I always feel a sense of satisfaction from understanding an author's choice of words and his reasons for writing the text, especially as they often offer an insight into ancient thought and politics.

It is commonly thought that a strong and unique opening line is a good way to catch the eye of the admissions tutor. This can certainly be true, and given the sheer number of statements which tutors have to read year on year, this approach can be quite refreshing. This particular student uses a quote from a rather unusual source for Classics; modern fiction literature, which immediately attracts attention. More importantly, however, he goes on to explain how this progressed further for him as an individual, tackling both *genuine interest* and *dedication* in one paragraph.

An aspect of the Classics course that excites me is its broad scope, which affords me both the unique opportunity of exploring two whole civilizations and the chance to specialize in investigating their literary works. Having studied a collection of both epic and prose Latin texts (Virgil's Aeneid Book IV *and Ovid's* Metamorphoses Book VIII *amongst them), I am looking forward to broadening the range of Latin authors I shall encounter and deepening my understanding of Classical culture and linguistic style. While analysing* In Catilinam Book 1 *for AS-level Latin, I consolidated my knowledge of the orator Cicero and his career as a Roman politician by reading Robert Harris's* Imperium, *a fascinating novel which brought to my attention the importance of rhetoric as a refined skill and art, and informed me about the state of Roman politics at the time. I have especially enjoyed drawing parallels between the orations of Cicero and those of US president Barack Obama, who employs similar rhetorical devices to his ancient predecessor in his speeches.*

This next section demonstrates significant innovation, first recounting the various readings the student has undertaken as part of his studies, but more importantly linking it to further, contemporary reading which is outside his remit. He also demonstrates good intellectual ingenuity by applying the principles of his study to current affairs.

I am particularly keen to investigate aspects of Ancient Greek civilization, where my interest is likely to lie in its literature and history. As a good introduction to Greek literature, I have recently moved on to reading the translation of Homer's Odyssey, something I have found hugely rewarding and which has enabled me to draw comparisons between Greek and Roman styles in Classical epic literature.

One of the key characteristics that defines an *unsatisfied intellectual curiosity* is a prospective element: someone who is not being pushed to his maximum will be looking ahead to greater challenges. This paragraph gives the feeling of someone who is well researched in the content of the Oxbridge course, and is already raring to embark on his degree.

All my sixth-form subjects should, I feel, serve as a good preparation for a Classics degree. My study of both Latin and English at A Level has taught me something about literary criticism as well as the importance of being selective, qualitative and concise in my writing. I have learned from Mathematics and Physics to approach problems in an analytical, measured and rational manner. After attending several Classics lectures in the past year, I have also become aware of the significance of being willing to embrace different interpretations of matters, rather than being dogmatic and single-minded.

You will find that most subjects at A level will lend some value to the course which you are about to embark on; show how this is the case, so that your particular portfolio of study becomes a strong method to support your future studies.

My extracurricular activities have, I believe, helped to develop integral educational and life skills. Having represented the school in badminton, cricket and football, I have discovered the value of teamwork and of building relationships within these respective teams. My selection as a school prefect has given me an added sense of responsibility to serve as a positive role model to other students. My participation at the school Mencap Funday has alerted me to the courage and strength of those living lives very different from my own, as has my role as house charity representative. Moreover, as a viola player in the school symphony orchestra and having twice had the privilege to perform at the prestigious Barbican concert hall, I have realized the significance of striking a balance between academic and extracurricular pursuits.

The extracurricular paragraph of your personal statement is critically important because it is relatively short compared to the academic, but must convey the sense of *potential* by the quality and quantity of your achievements.

*I understand how much of a privilege it is to be able to further my study of
Classics at an institution with fine educational resources, and I believe that
I am prepared for the rigours of university life.*

Closing sentences are sometimes difficult to construct in a way that is more sophisticated than 'I am looking forward to studying subject X at Cambridge', but this student manages to work in one more key element to round off his personal statement: humility. Having read hundreds of personal statements, I know that many students sound like they believe they *deserve* a place, and all the advantages and benefits that come with it, simply because they are talented and able. This particular student avoids doing that and is respectful of the privilege that is higher education. He places a focus rightly back on his studies after discussion of extracurricular affairs, and demonstrates knowledge of one of the advantages of Oxbridge, namely the '*fine educational resources*'.

Structure 2 – natural development of interest

This personal statement type follows a different structure to the above and is based around your intellectual curiosity, which is likely to stem in part from your school subjects and then develop from there. Start with these subjects, and highlight particular areas which fascinate you: achievements, presentations or projects that show a high achievement in this area.

On this foundation, you can then go on to discuss your extra academic pursuits, discussing additional reading, courses and activities you have undertaken to further your original interest. The advantage of this method is that it is easy to follow, has a solid basis and develops the *commitment* and *dedication* characteristics very well.

The main disadvantage is that some consider it a 'slow starter' – it is not as eye-catching as openings involving more exotic and extracurricular content. However, as more and more students opt for a structure-1 approach, you may find opportunities to shine in the middle of your personal statement, as you can demonstrate how you built on your A-level work to demonstrate *unsatisfied intellectual curiosity*.

Example 3 – Medicine (Cambridge)

*My enthusiasm for medicine was sparked by a curiosity for understanding
science and how the human body works, leading me to consider a career as
a doctor. I enjoy the challenges of Chemistry, Biology and Mathematics at A level,
which have allowed me to see the molecular, physiological and quantitative
relationships of processes in our lives, giving me a variety of approaches when
considering how humans and their environment interact and therefore how we
can improve the lives of ourselves and others.*

This student manages to neatly sum up the principles of her A-level subjects in a succinct and innovative manner, which helps to maintain the impact of her opening paragraph even though it is following a structure-2 format. The real strength, however, comes in the next paragraph.

> *However, I have also felt that I wanted to explore more than the school curricula, and sought out science courses, including a Pharmacology master class at Cambridge University, Aspirin synthesis course at Bristol University, Forensic sciences course at Huddersfield University and several others to extend and supplement what I had learnt at school. Whilst I know that the synthesis of pharmaceuticals is not part of the medical course, I hope that my enthusiasm for studying various aspects of it certainly is. I undertook an Open University course, 'Human genetics and health issues', which I studied independently and which fuelled my growing interest in genetics, encouraging me to read* Mutants *by Armand Leroi and* The Language of the Genes *by Steve Jones, deepening my fascination with how genes are expressed and their impact on the growing embryo. In Religious Studies at A level, I have had to write extensively on controversial medical issues, learning how to draw my own conclusions after careful consideration of many philosophical viewpoints.*

This paragraph shows exactly what you can achieve with a structure-2 format: an undiluted showcase of great intellectual pursuits which are beyond those demanded at A level. In this case, University-led practical courses and additional Open University modules coupled with some interest-based reading give an impressive account of this student's academic drive. It also maintains the momentum of the statement, which is the opposite of structure 1, which starts off in an exciting manner but must inevitably come back to A-level discussion, which is somewhat less appealing than your innovative and independent activities.

> *This interest is tempered by a genuine enjoyment of human interaction and a desire to do humanitarian work. I believe medicine has these elements titrated in the perfect proportions of compassion, dedication and communication skills with a passion for knowledge and teamwork.*
>
> *With this in mind, my motivation for medicine has been strongly reaffirmed through work experience, showing me the reality of medicine, especially in the paediatric unit at Manchester Royal Infirmary, where I saw some of the hardships alongside the rewarding highlights of life as a doctor. The most valuable experience was simply spending time on the wards, speaking to doctors and other MDT members, seeing how they handled the challenges*

of dealing with patients, explaining diagnoses and reassuring families, as the dynamics of paediatric consultations were very different from adult consultations I observed in North Manchester General Hospital and Papworth Hospital. A week of cardiothoracic surgery at Wythenshawe was an unforgettable experience. Mitral and aortic valve replacements and coronary artery bypass grafts were fascinating as the surgeon described the anatomy of the patient during surgery. Seeing the patient improve almost immediately afterwards was immensely gratifying.

One of the key features discussed in this chapter is the importance of demonstrating good written communication skills as part of your overall profile via your UCAS form. In this case, the student manages to incorporate scientific terminology comfortably, both by showing her understanding (that anatomy, the study of the structures of the body, is concerned with physical manifestations such as the heart valves and coronary arteries), as well as in innovative ways, such as '*medicine has these elements titrated in the perfect proportions of compassion, dedication and communication skills*'. Try to use scientific, literary or rhetorical devices in such interesting ways to generate appeal in more mundane sections of your statement.

I have learnt to organize and prioritize by balancing schoolwork and other academic pursuits with leading and participating in school orchestras and working for Grade 8 in both violin and public speaking. Applying my public speaking skills in debate camp with ESU was new and stimulating as I adapted to different audiences to communicate better and more efficiently. Volunteering at a disabled children's charity, PHAB, gave me a priceless experience of attending to the personal needs of a group of children and I have been awarded two v-fifty awards, for over 180 hours of volunteering with them and an elderly people's home. Rowing for school, being part of a team under pressure in three head races and regattas, has been very enjoyable. Representing school in the regional finals of the RSC Chemistry competition was the culmination of my school experiences, bringing together teamwork, communication skills and the application of scientific knowledge.

This student benefits from a well-planned extracurricular activities spectrum; in particular she combines a number of 'high-density' activities such as passing musical exams, and a significant quantitative commitment in volunteering. Interestingly, she saves the RSC Chemistry competition for the finale of her achievements, and again this helps to take the focus back to the academic side, and reassures the admissions tutors that despite her numerous interests and talents, the primary focus for her at university really is her studies.

I am eager to take on the challenge of studying Medicine at university, building on my current analytical skills whilst acquiring a new knowledge base and approach to scientific and patient-orientated problems.

As with the previous personal statement, the student demonstrates more than simple eagerness; she also acknowledges the limits of her own abilities and looks forward to improving herself. It is also clear that she appreciates the difference between school learning, which is systems based, compared to university-level education, which is patient based; this again adds to the impression of a well-prepared, realistic and ambitious student.

Structural variations

Innovative students have tried different personal statement formats to add something new as well as demonstrate their flair with written communication skills. Students have opted for a chronological structure, a list of key attributes for medicine or an 'atomic' structure with a central core and several clouds of possibilities and probabilities for their future. One very adventurous applicant decided to end their extracurricular description of their interest in poetry in a haiku.

As with any novel strategy, there is always a risk. It may be difficult to follow or end up not communicating all of the essential information. Remember that the personal statement is the vehicle to get you to the interview stage, and therefore you do not wish to miss that opportunity by coming across as too arrogant. Nevertheless, interesting structures and content say a great deal about the explorative and innovative mind of a student and can reflect well. My advice to those of you who are experimenting is to gain as much feedback as possible to ensure that your statement is comprehensible and has the impact that you intended.

Summary

- The personal statement is a vehicle for expressing your unique academic and personal history.

- Remember to cover the key characteristics of passion, intellectual curiosity, commitment, innovation, ability and potential.

- Written communication skills are very important; use this opportunity to showcase them.

- Consider structure 1 to create a strong and eye-catching opening.

- Structure 2 has a more progressive description of your interest.

- Be as brave or as cautious as you dare with structure, but make sure that it is easy to follow your thought processes.

- You must focus on academics as the main content.

- Extracurricular activities complement these but should be towards the end so as not to steal focus.

CHAPTER 8

How to get a teacher reference

- The importance of the teacher reference
- Research
- Building your reference
- Approaching your referring teacher
- What teachers say

The importance of the teacher reference

The role of school support in a successful application cannot be overstated. Imagine for a moment that you are an admissions tutor and you have two wonderful candidates with equal grades and personal statements. Whom will you want to call for interview – the person with a general supportive reference or the one with a glowing and exceptional teacher report? For all the time students spend on their personal statements, this area can gain you a large advantage over your peers simply because they are not aware of how they can influence it.

Secondly, admissions tutors are sensitive to small nuances in the language of your references. Several tutors that I have interviewed say that most teachers will never indicate negative thoughts in an obvious way such as 'This student has a poor attendance record.' They will at most give vague allusions to a problem, eg 'This student produces good work when it is on time.' Therefore, small differences in the language used give very different impressions to tutors, and the threshold of losing or gaining ground on your competitors is also small. It is therefore vital to use this chapter to optimize your chances of success.

Research

The first step, as with all aspects of your application, is finding out who is writing your reference and how it is compiled. I suggest the best resource for this is actually your seniors from school rather than the teachers themselves. This is because you do not want to appear to artificially change the way your reference is written; rather, the method of improving your outcome is more subtle than by directly requesting your teacher to write wonderful things about you.

There are many variations between schools as to how they construct a reference and each requires its own approach. Common methods include:

- collating the reports from your various subject teachers and form tutor;

- asking you to fill in a form stating your achievements and goals;

- discussing with the student directly about what they wish to put in their statement and what they wish to be mentioned in the reference.

You are best off asking your seniors in school or who have just graduated about exactly what the process of creating their teacher reference was. Try to get in touch with any Oxbridge school alumni; you may find they are quite willing to help you with feedback on other areas of your application such as college selection and interview practice. (You may be able to obtain their contact details via your school careers department if you have one, or teachers in charge of Oxbridge or university applications.)

Building your reference

A good impression is built up over time. The most important step is that you start working on this *immediately* after reading this chapter. Take on board the advice and make the necessary changes to your activities in order to maximize your Oxbridge application:

- You should arrive promptly to school every single day without fail. Any deficits in this arena can be taken to indicate a lax attitude to scholarship and academia. The trick here is to avoid any negative impression which may hurt your reference, rather than having any additional benefit per se; this is quite reasonable as you are expected to be on time anyway.

- You should be neat and tidy in your appearance and attire. The idea of an academic outlook is that you are at school to study, not to socialize or waltz down a catwalk. If you look serious about your studies, you will give that impression to people who meet you. This does not mean you cannot be expressive or creative in what you do – but whatever you choose to wear, keep it outside the framework of 'looking like a scruff'.

- Avoid arrogance at all costs. This is hugely important, and many teachers that I have spoken to who are referees for Oxbridge applications find this a huge turnoff when they come to put pen to paper. It can make a teacher not want to give their utmost to support an intolerable but otherwise brilliant student. Some methods of avoiding this are:
  - Do not repeatedly refer to your achievements or activities.
  - Do not try to use 'proxy' methods of informing your teacher. A proxy method is talking about an activity or achievement you have undertaken to, for example, a fellow student, whilst in earshot of the teacher, for the purpose of having them overhear. It is much less subtle than you think, and is both annoying and rude.
  - Diversify your conversation. Your referring teacher may get very tired of discussing your university application every day. Try to introduce 'regular' conversation into your routine, be it about current events, weather, *Britain's Got Talent* or whichever topic you prefer.

- Hand in all assignments to a high standard and on time. A consistently high level of academic performance on your homework reflects your ability and aptitude for independent scholastic endeavours. This is one of the ways you can reflect on your dedication to your subject.

- Participate appropriately and intelligently in class. It is important to play an active role in class discussions and topics; teachers will not be able to see the wonderful and insightful thoughts in your head if you do not express them in class. Try to gauge your participation relative to your peers – you do not want to be far below the average for the group; however, you also want to avoid being an incessant bore by dominating all conversations and having your hand up all the time. This will also reduce your ability to learn by listening to input by others.

- Remember to take on board feedback and criticisms in a constructive way – this is another significant learning activity which you should be seen to be able to do. This type of balanced, active participation is most likely to benefit your reference via an indirect route – through subject-teacher reports which are collated by your referee. However, if your referee is also one of your subject teachers, you should be doubly sure that your approach is intelligent, measured and active.

- Prepare for your classes. Try and get an idea of the topic lists for upcoming weeks and do a little pre-reading. This will enable you to avoid feeling pressured during the class environment and allow you to cement concepts in your mind, rather than discovering them for the first time. Furthermore, this will help you to feel more comfortable in 'live-action' academic discussions, which will be helpful for performance at interview.

- Go above and beyond the requirements of your course within school subjects. This can be one of the hardest things to make yourself do, as most students feel that it is an optimal solution to cut corners and focus on their application. However, the extra benefits which are described in the section below should convince you of why this is not always a good idea.

- The *extended project* is one method to gain an in-depth understanding of a particular subject, and this can double up as an interesting point of discussion at interview. Finding out about this early on can help you plan for a worthwhile topic of study; last-minute decisions can result in spending time on a topic that you are not that interested in or is far more time consuming than you had anticipated.

- Actively search for opportunities in academia rather than waiting for people to tell you. There are often writing, essay or other competitions for students which may be accessible to you. There may be some activities in school such as writing an article for a school magazine or paper; you can tailor this to your advantage by covering a topic on the subject of your application: perhaps an in-depth discussion on recent political events or on a recent scientific breakthrough.

Additional advantages

Working on gaining a top reference is a very *efficient* activity to undertake. You do not have to go out of your way to do it as it is conducted entirely in school. It takes advantage of your current academic and extracurricular activities, which again you will already be undertaking. It costs very little in terms of time but requires a degree of intelligence and social skills. You will have to optimize your academic performance both in terms of written work and classroom participation; this will have secondary benefits including AS-level module marks, subject understanding for interview and improving technique for sample written work.

There may be a time when you can reasonably reduce your school-level activities, that is, during preparation for interview and the aptitude test phase. This is typically early on in your A2 or final school year, and gives you some time to catch up. However, bear in mind that the topics you will cover can still be useful at interview, and also that falling behind on schoolwork is inadvisable in the era of the A* requirement. See the Tip box below for an ideal strategy for coping with your schoolwork during this period.

The summer before your UCAS application is a golden opportunity which most students miss out on. The first thing to say is that I'm afraid it is not a real holiday; of course, you must give yourself some time to unwind after your summer examinations, but serious Oxbridge students have a large number of tasks. Participating in worthwhile extracurricular activities and personal statement drafting are the mainstay of your occupation, but the most astute students will spend some time *looking ahead to the A2-level material* which you will be covering in the autumn term. Why? This is because this period is simply the busiest, most stressful time that you will encounter in your school career, bar none. Oxbridge applicants have far more to do than non-Oxbridge applicants, and these demands, in addition to your schoolwork, can make this a difficult period to navigate successfully. Furthermore, stress can have a negative impact on your health, the quality of your work and, most important, on your creativity and freedom of thinking – which are exactly what you will need come interview time.

Therefore, taking the pressure off this time in advance is one of the best strategic moves you can make over the summer period. Don't use up all your time on it, but doing some work every day adds up to a vast amount by the end of your holidays.

There is one final upside: in order to gain the information about what you will cover next year, you will need to consult your teachers. This will therefore be another way to demonstrate your keenness, determination and organization, which will add even further value to your reference.

Overall, the school reference is by far the least publicized aspect of your overall application, which makes it an even more vital one for you. Do not ignore this opportunity to fairly, genuinely and simply gain a large advantage over your competitors.

Approaching your referring teacher

Be open in discussing your application and reference with your teacher. The best way to do this is to seek advice rather than meeting your teacher just to tell them about all the wonderful things you have been doing. One approach is to bring them a question from some of your additional reading. For example, you may have been reading a *New Scientist* article on the role of adenosine release as a mechanism for acupuncture. You might ask them about how adenosine normally plays a role in human biology, and then discuss the implications of this new finding. You may have recently been moved by watching the films of Pedro Almodovar as part of your investigation of Spanish cinema. You might discuss what your teacher thought of his films, and what other directors he might recommend both to further your interest and to contrast with it as well.

It can be useful to engage teachers on a more personal level and ask them about their own interests or what inspired them to study at university level. For all teachers who are Oxbridge graduates, it can be helpful for you to hear about their experiences at the university itself, and no doubt they will have an interesting tale or two about their time in higher education. You can learn about their application experience and interview questions too.

Try to engage teachers with a question rather than a request or demand. You will both be accustomed to the roles of student asking for information and teacher giving it and thereafter mutually engaging in discussion. Reversing these roles may make the situation feel, subconsciously or otherwise, unusual and make the interaction more difficult than it should be.

For example: 'I'm currently taking an Open University course to extend my interest in genetics. Do you have any advice on extra reading that can help me with this course as well as my general understanding of genetics?'

This is preferable to: 'I'm taking an additional course in genetics via the Open University. Do you think you can put this in my teacher reference because I don't have enough room in my UCAS form?' (This was an actual approach used by an enthusiastic but rather unsavvy student.)

It is important to be sensitive to your teacher's responses and time. Try not to outstay your welcome, and politely excuse yourself when you feel your time is up. Do not assume that a teacher will have time for a lengthy talk if you randomly collar them in the corridor; this is at best unlikely and at worst outright rude. Instead, try to book an appointment with them for a fixed time in advance, eg 'Could I meet with you next Wednesday after school for 20 minutes or so for some advice about my Oxbridge application, please?' This way, the teacher has a chance to plan for the event and suggest alternatives if they are busy. Furthermore, introducing the element of a time limit gives a boundary to your interaction and avoids the teacher seeing you as a potential black hole of infinite questions.

You should not expect your teacher to remember everything you have said or done at a meeting, so make it easy for them. Prepare a short and to-the-point A4 sheet with a list of your activities and achievements or e-mail it to them. They will find it a helpful resource to draw upon when writing your reference, and it will also help ensure that they don't miss out any key points unintentionally. Use structure (eg putting the most important things first) or formatting (*limited* use of eg bold font) to draw attention to important points.

What teachers say

It's easy to write a reference. I think of the immediate impression of what comes to mind with a student, and put it down in black and white. Dedicated, hardworking, bright and innovative students act a certain way, others who are experts in bluffing and fluffing are also easy to spot.

One of the problems I find with potential Oxbridge students is their attitude. They feel like they are somehow entitled to extra help on tap just because they are applying to a top uni. Arrogant students are the ones that don't go as far as their overinflated egos might think they will.

You don't have to find the best students – they find you, and show you directly and indirectly why they are exceptional and hard-working talents of the future.

Summary

- Getting an exceptional teacher reference is a commonly overlooked area for applications.

- It can lend a considerable, independent advantage to your chances of success.

- There is no quick solution; it takes hard work and attention.

- Punctuality, participation, attire and consistency all have a role to play.

- It is not your teacher's duty to research all your activities; make it easy for them and let them know what you are doing.

- Be polite and considerate of your teacher's time.

CHAPTER 9

Sample written work submission and aptitude test essays

- Why is this so vital?
- Handwriting and written communication skills
- Writing a good essay
- Worked example

Submitting examples of your written work is another important step in your application. As with your UCAS form, you can put in carefully considered effort and you are not under the same time pressures as the interview, pre-interview tests or aptitude tests. This chapter details how to get maximum value out of an often overlooked part of your Oxbridge package. However, it is important to stress that the principles contained within this chapter are critical for every applicant, as they apply to interview questions and preparation in a very similar way.

In addition, the principles of excellent written work extend to aptitude tests, which will be laid out in Chapter 10, as many of these will include an essay question as part of the assessment. This chapter covers the essay segment, including how to maximize your performance specifically for the aptitude test, and this includes an extended example of how to use critical appraisal, diverse examples and flawless logic to construct an outstanding essay.

Why is this so vital?

Assessment in almost all subjects in Oxbridge contains an element of essay writing, and therefore skills in this area are considered highly by admissions tutors. This is because essays require fluid written communication skills, excellent organization and both positive and negative selection: what to include and what not to include. They are the primary method of assessment for many subjects, including traditional 'essay' subjects in the arts and humanities, but the social and natural scientists will also find that they too are given plenty of essays to write. Written work of greater length, in the form of dissertations, also have a large role to play in the later years. It is for this reason that admissions tutors wish to assess your ability to undertake these tasks at a school level first, by looking at your submitted written work.

Sample written work submission

For Oxford, essays are required for most of the humanities subjects, which are:

- Archaeology and Anthropology (including Classical);
- Classics (including with English, Modern Languages and Oriental Studies);
- English and Modern Languages;
- English Literature and Language;
- Geography;
- History (including with Economics, English, Politics and Modern Languages);
- History of Art;
- Modern Languages;
- Music;
- Oriental Studies;
- Philosophy (including with Modern Languages and Theology).

For Cambridge:

- Anglo-Saxon, Norse and Celtic;
- Asian and Middle Eastern Studies;
- Classics;
- Education;
- English;
- Geography;
- History;
- History of Art;
- Law (note – this is not required at Oxford);
- Linguistics;
- Modern Languages;
- Music;
- Philosophy;
- Politics, Psychology and Sociology;
- Theology.

Deadlines for written work submission tend to be in November but you *must* check the Oxford and Cambridge websites as this varies by subject as well as university.

It is important to note that your submission cannot be a piece which is specifically written for your application; it must be part of your schoolwork and marked by a teacher. Although this theoretically limits your options, there are several ways to help yourself gain better marks as long as you are willing to plan ahead, and these are discussed below:

- Do plan in advance. Look up the deadlines and ensure that you will have time to make enough effort to get your best piece of written work submitted.

- Talk to your teachers. Mention your need for submitted written work for your application and ask what assignments might be coming up in the next few weeks. You may be able to plan ahead more thoroughly and put more effort into it with advanced planning and research.

- Try to peak at the right time and give yourself some time to draft, redraft and finally create a well-refined and reviewed piece of work.

Handwriting and written communication skills

Legibility is clearly the absolute minimum standard for your written work – the marking tutors will not be impressed by having a scrawl to decipher from you each week if you are admitted to their college. Further than this level, neatness is desirable for a college academic who may end up marking your work on a weekly basis for at least one of your years! Take your time whilst producing your written work, and make sure it is pristine. Many students are now opting to type their work. This has some advantages and disadvantages. In favour of it, you will be guaranteed to have very clear and presentable work that will make life easier for the admissions team. However, the downside is that they cannot see how you write, and therefore you are unable to score any 'additional' points if your presentation is of a high quality. Therefore the advantage of handwriting your submission is that it gives you the chance to showcase how you will be working week on week in the Oxbridge environment, and if it is very good, it will give you a slight advantage. The main value of essays is, of course, in the content, but do not underestimate the value of first impressions; having an untidy essay is the written equivalent of turning up for interview with your shirt untucked and hair scruffy – avoid this at all costs.

> You may need to make photocopies of your written work for submission; remember that black ink photocopies much better than blue!

For aptitude tests, all the points above become even more important. You will most certainly be under time pressure, if not for the physical writing, then more so for the planning and synthesizing examples. Ensure that you practise writing in a large, legible manner in exam conditions; each year several tutors say they have to ignore some examples and paragraphs in students' aptitude tests because they are simply incomprehensible. This is the worst possible way of shooting your academic self in the foot; do not fall into this trap!

Writing a good essay

What to focus on

The main characteristics of a good Oxbridge essay are as follows: *structure*, *depth*, *breadth and innovation*, and *critical appraisal*. I will address each of them in turn, and you should make sure you address each of these issues in any of your written submissions.

Structure

A good essay structure is vital to impressing admissions tutors for several reasons. First, it demonstrates a key understanding of the subject at hand. This is because you must organize your material within the essay and the order of what you choose to discuss, and its quantity, reflect on the intellectual choices that you have made. It becomes very clear whether you are knowledgeable or just using fillers to complete your assignment. The introduction plays a key role, and this should map out what you will cover during the essay, in a succinct and economical manner. In fact, one Oxbridge tutor says that he can identify a top or mediocre student from the introduction, and the rest of the reading is just to confirm this original assertion. Make the job easy for your markers by indicating how the rest of their reading will pan out.

The conclusion is also an important part of the structure, summing up what has been said, but it also a good ground for innovation, and so it will be covered in a later section.

Structure checklist:

Introduction. Does your introduction both reflect the layout of your essay and give the reader a clear idea of where you will be tackling each of your arguments?

Proportions. Is your essay evenly balanced? Have you given due coverage to important issues and mentioned less important ones in brief?

Sequence. Within each section, have you discussed the more common or prominent things early on and rare events later on? (See Tip box below.)

Signposting. Do you give verbal and structural indications that you are changing topic? Make new paragraphs to indicate change, and use signposts such as 'on the other hand', 'additionally', 'in contrast' and so on.

Subheadings. Where appropriate, make use of subheadings to texture your writing and make it easier and less monotonous to follow. Try to keep these titles short and punchy; elaborate on them in the material below rather than in the title itself.

Plan. Writing a good plan is the framework for achieving all of these goals. It can be easily done for your submitted essays where you have time to prepare, and can help you to perform all the checks above before you even get going.

I would encourage you to create plans even when you have an essay under timed conditions, as you will gain the large advantage of seeing the overall picture of the essay, how to structure it and where to add innovation as necessary.

'COMMON THINGS ARE COMMON'

One of the Cambridge admissions tutors whom I spoke to about this book told me of his frustration with 'brilliant students who are somewhat lacking in common sense'. The particular example was when he read an essay on the reasons for the fall of the Roman Empire. The student opened with a very compelling, detailed paragraph on the suspicion of extraterrestrial involvement, as researched by a prominent Californian professor of Archaeology, due to several aptly described inconsistencies between historians which could not be explained: the so called 'irrational' phenomena. The student then described the invention of the horseshoe in Germania as being a key technological advance which facilitated the invasion of the Empire. Only at this stage did he move on to explaining the other more commonly held reasons such as civil unrest and political instability.

The tutor presented me with the student's work and said, 'As you can see, this student is quite innovative and clearly well read. However, common things are common, and aliens are not. Don't you think he should have perhaps saved this for the end, after giving me a bit more substance?' I may not have read Classics, but I certainly did do A-level Latin, and I am inclined to agree with my more learned colleague.

This principle also applies to many other subjects. In history, when describing the causes of the First World War, it might not be prudent to open with A J P Taylor's railroad timetable theory, which states that the great powers were committed to advanced decisions because of the reliance on trains for mass transport. It may be better to first describe the formation of mutual defence alliances, the growing influence of nationalism and imperialist activity in Africa and Asia as areas of contention for European countries, before introducing this idea into the mix.

Similarly, if describing the causes of heart disease, it is not the best idea to start with the rare genetic disorder of dextrocardia, where the heart appears on the right-hand side of the body rather than the left, as part of Katagener's syndrome. Try starting with coronary heart disease and its risk factors such as smoking, high blood pressure, high cholesterol and diabetes.

Always remember, *common things are common*, and demonstrate your quantitative understanding of this by discussing it first, before moving on to the more unusual.

Depth

Depth is the next most important issue when it comes to essay writing for Oxbridge. How can we demonstrate depth of knowledge? The best and most effective way is often by using and explaining examples. For example (and here I am demonstrating my own depth of knowledge), it is not enough simply to mention Pareto efficiency and Pareto improvements when describing the political and economic ramifications of government educational initiatives. Try to explain it using a three-step method as follows:

(1) Pareto efficiency describes a situation where someone cannot make gains without another person suffering. (2) For example, if there is only one type of good in the world which people want, then the world will be Pareto efficient because for someone to benefit, someone else must lose. However, if there are multiple goods, and people have different desires, then Pareto improvements can occur when a man who likes fish, but has chicken, gives his good away to a chicken lover and receives fish in return. This way both parties benefit with no real loss and therefore the system was not yet Pareto efficient. (3) The UK's policy on investment in education and employment support for the lower socio-economic groups has the effect of improving their prospects for future employment and diminishing crime within these populations, whilst at the same time reducing costs of the better-off by lowering prison costs and dependency on benefit, which could therefore represent a Pareto improvement. However, this improvement will only occur if the costs incurred by the investment are matched by the savings.

Looking at this essay segment, the author undertakes three different tasks. In step 1, he briefly explains the theory, fact or phenomenon. However, this is not enough to convince the Oxbridge tutor that you fully understand what is mean by the term; in fact, many students are able to memorize definitions and regurgitate them onto paper. Therefore step 2 involves using an example which demonstrates your deep understanding of the topic. This can often involve *simplification* or *application* to real-world situations, as this shows you can take a complex principle and really make it relevant to yourself and your essay. Step 3 is the final area where you bring the theory together with your essay, and link it directly to addressing the question.

Showing off the depth of your knowledge will help you to stand out from the crowd and gain the admissions tutor's interest. That interest will translate to wanting to speak to you at interview to see how deep your knowledge really goes, and then inviting you to study at their college to add even more depth.

Breadth and innovation

The other important characteristic of a good essay is breadth and innovation. These are considered together because they are both very alike; they both require thinking outside the box, in ways which are not common to other students. Consider the following problem. Essays often fall into one of two categories; either a *long and thin* essay which has lots of depth but not much breadth, or a *short and fat* essay which has plenty of different examples but fails to explain any of them in depth. This is what makes essay writing such a challenge.

How do we generate breadth? The best way to demonstrate this is the type of example that you choose to include, which also gives an innovative feel by applying unusual or uncommon points to a problem. Consider the following examples when writing an essay about the history of scientific discovery:

Parallel examples. These types of example are those which are similar to your main example. For example, if your main (and therefore more detailed) example is Alexander Fleming and his careless treatment of petri dishes, which gave rise to the discovery of penicillin, you can also mention in brief other accidental discoveries such as Wilson Greatbach's implantable pacemaker, or list some in the next, more linked, example below.

Intra-topic examples. The next way to branch out is to look for examples within your own subject. For example, if you are a biological scientist, you can think of more biologically relevant examples to weave into your essay.

If you are using short examples to help demonstrate your *breadth*, it can help the flow of your essay if you can find efficient ways of linking examples together. For example: 'Constantin Fahlberg discovered saccharin ($C_7H_5NO_3S$) by bringing home the compound on his hands when working on coal tar and finding that his wife's rolls were sweeter. Ignaz Semmelweiss reduced death rates in surgery by washing hands after post mortems and thus "discovered" the importance of hand hygiene. Perhaps it is fortunate that the two did not work together.'

Extra-subject examples. Finally, it can be very helpful to look well outside your discipline to other fields. In this case, the author of the essay concluded: 'Living things are not the only things to suffer from randomness, and researcher Jamie Link discovered "smart dust" when she accidentally exploded a silicon chip but found that the resulting fragments still functioned as sensors.'

There are many such examples, and it is always worth looking outside the box for these ideas. In order to help you 'discover' this breadth, there are some activities you can undertake that can facilitate this aspect of your essay.

One of the tools you can use is the subject axis table in Chapter 12. This will indicate which topics or subjects are relatively close to one another, and therefore might be a good place to start whilst thinking about examples. It is certainly common for Physics to draw upon Mathematics, Computer Sciences and Engineering for examples. Likewise, English Literature students can make use of examples and tools from fields as varied as Linguistics, Psychology and History. As you progress, you will begin to think about these subjects as you write the essay itself, and always have one eye on how they can affect the way you shape an excellent, well-rounded, balanced essay.

You are unlikely to find the breadth of examples in your day-to-day AS- and A-level reading, in a manner that is relevant to your subject. Therefore, for this particular aspect of your essay writing, this is where the value of additional reading really comes into play. Refer to Chapters 4 and 5 to discover strategies on how to diversify your reading portfolio and gain the maximum advantage for essay writing as well as interview answers. One of the key principles of the Oxbridge application is that almost no reading is ever 'wasted' as long as it is of a good intellectual level. You will be surprised at how quickly you develop a wide repertoire of sources to draw upon.

The other principle that has been a theme throughout the book is the importance of keeping a record of this additional reading. You should continually add examples to your file or portfolio each week as you continue towards the later stages of your Oxbridge applications, particularly building up to interview. It is important to store them as 'functional': try to use the example above in the *depth* section to write out steps 1 and 2 for each example. As you can imagine, step 3 would not be possible to predict – you will have to adapt your examples to the question in hand. Finally, try not to overextend yourself; make sure that the examples you are using are relevant to the title, and although there is plenty of scope to make connections using argument, some students can take this too far and use irrelevant examples. Avoid this mistake by constantly referring back to the title.

Critical analysis

Critical analysis is an important skill to demonstrate. Even if you have been carefully applying the rules above and have an excellent structure, with good depth and range of examples, you need to showcase your ability to look at the information you have presented with a critical eye. Consider the following example, used by a Veterinary Sciences applicant when addressing the essay topic 'Describe the value of human–animal interactions.'

An experiment conducted in depressed patients found that swimming with dolphins served as an effective treatment for depression when compared to medication. The study was conducted over the course of a month with daily swimming sessions, and the dolphin-treatment group showed significant improvements in their reported mood (subjective) and observed mood (objective). However, the flaws in this study mean that I cannot rely on this to demonstrate that animal interactions are curative for depression, for the following reasons. First, dolphin treatments could only take place on a tropical island but recruits were from the UK. Therefore, the difference in weather could have made a significant impact, and this has a well-established basis from studies in Seasonal Affective Disorder (SAD). Second, the effect of swimming also meant that patients had one hour of exercise per day for a month, which may also have contributed to the effect of increased mood, which the medication group did not have. In order to study this, we would need to compare a group who swam for one hour per day without dolphins. Finally, the time required for effective therapy of antidepressant medications is more than one month to reach peak effect, but for financial reasons the dolphin therapy could only continue for that long. Therefore, we are only comparing this therapy to the early stages of antidepressant medication, and not the maximum effect of medication.

This student achieves many goals in this single paragraph. First, she has chosen a rather unusual study to address in the essay; this demonstrates her *breadth and innovation*. However, vitally she goes beyond this to critically appraise her own example, shows the value and the flaws in it, and her final interpretation is carefully considered. She makes good use of *technical terminology* whilst at the same time making it clear that she understands the principles in lay language, and finally makes suggestions as to how to overcome the problems she has noted.

This is an excellent way to show the admissions tutors that you are ready for an Oxbridge education; they do not want students who will simply take information at face value and remember it; they wish to see how you interpret it and whether or not you can be critical of it. In any subject, be it Literature, Social Sciences or Humanities, this skill is of paramount importance and you should make sure that you demonstrate this within your essay to place it a cut above the rest.

I hope you can start to see the level of sophistication which is required when it comes to the art and science of essay writing. The good news is that this type of careful analysis comes with practice. However, that is also the bad news, and you must put in plenty of effort and be prepared to get it wrong sometimes in the build-up to your final submission piece. Apart from your own internal assessment, feedback from others is vitally important and that is also covered below.

Worked example

This example gives you an insight into the level of expectation on yourself as the author of the essay; the sheer depth and amount of critical thought that must go into your submission are very considerable. However, please note that the skills you will develop in this arena will go on to benefit you greatly at interview. Furthermore, if you can find peers, teachers, tutors or Oxbridge graduates to review your essay, you will continue to learn, develop and improve, so that your final submitted piece represents the best that you can achieve.

Question: 'Superheroes as a super problem: discuss, with examples, how the powers of superheroes and supervillains may be possible in scientific terms.'

There are many different things we associate with superhumans, whether they have hidden human identities, whether they are heroes or villains or whether they had been bitten by spiders, but one thing that we agree on is that superhumans have super powers. They have an infinite range of powers from super strength to flight, all which seem impossible.

Super strength would be a good place to start as, unlike other powers, humans have some degree of strength. So this superpower is just an extension of a human capability. Therefore, if we just enhance what gives humans strength, we would be able to have super strength. As energy is released from cell metabolism and on an intracellular level, from mitochondria which makes ATP to give muscle cells the energy, to give the body strength, if there was a larger number of mitochondria and naturally a high metabolism, then the superhuman would have super strength.

However, if we look at a super power which isn't an enhancement of a human feature, then we can look at flight. As we do not possess anything that resembles flight, we can look at other creatures which do fly. As I look at birds, bats, flying squirrels and flying fish I see that they all have a large surface area in order to support the weight of the flying body. So, to keep as close to a human body as possible, the bones could be very light by being hollow in the middle like a bird's and, like a flying squirrel and a flying fish, there would be a large flap of skin between the torso and the arms to allow flight to occur, as the large surface area would make it possible for gliding and so catching air currents.

Yet some super powers will not be possible in the real world, such as telekineticity – being able to move objects with just the mind. This is because there has been no link at all between moving objects directly by just thinking that you want to move them.

Another superpower that can't be explained is the ability to spontaneously freeze objects as even if we had an area of the body that was below zero degrees centigrade, then we would need a long time in order to be able to freeze an object.

To conclude, I do not think that superhumans with super powers will ever be able to exist in the real world despite some people arguing that it could happen due to a mutation in the genetic code and then, from natural selection, that gene will become prevalent in the population, so allowing more chances for a superhero to be made. However, natural selection doesn't really happen any more due to humans having manipulated the environment to suit them, so there is hardly any difference between an advantageous phenotype and a disadvantageous phenotype, if it is anatomical or physiological. The only phenotype that will be advantageous is one that makes someone much cleverer than others as now we live in an age where humans excel in brain, not physical strength. Also, if that gene becomes prevalent in the population, then the 'super powers' will no longer be super.

Feedback

The point of this essay was to demonstrate to the examiner two main characteristics about yourself: that you have a very solid understanding of scientific principles; and that you can go beyond your current knowledge and apply these principles to events which are outside your knowledge. This type of process, know as the *extrapolated principle*, is one of the key criteria for selection in Oxbridge interviews, and I think you have been doing well so far in terms of your current knowledge, and I will be trying to push your boundaries a bit so that you can develop more skills in application.

Introduction

There are many different things we associate with superhumans, whether they have hidden human identities, whether they are heroes or villains or whether they had been bitten by spiders, but one thing that we agree on is that superhumans have super powers. They have an infinite range of powers from super strength to flight, all of which seem impossible.

This is a decent start to the problem, addressing the fact that of all the different characteristics of superheroes and supervillains, the main interest in terms of science would be their super powers. However, I would be tempted to include the following type of sentence after introductory sentences: 'I will focus on the science behind four main areas: super strength, flight, telekinetics and freezing.' This gives the reader some guidance as to the structure of the essay, and immediately adds a more organized air to the start.

Para 1

Super strength would be a good place to start as unlike other powers, humans have some degree of strength. So this superpower is just an extension of a human capability. Therefore, if we just enhance what gives humans strength, we would be able to have super strength. As energy is released from cell metabolism and on an intracellular level, from mitochondria which makes ATP to give muscle cells the energy, to give the body strength, if there was a larger number of mitochondria and naturally a high metabolism, then the superhuman would have super strength.

I think you have discussed the initial theory of your point well – super strength is simply a quantitative increase in normal strength, so looking at what gives a human strength is a good way to start. This is an example of the activity which I described in the preamble to this review – the *extrapolated principle*. I think your application of the knowledge here is a little off the mark – what you have discussed is energy production, which you have done well, and you have speculated that increasing energy would give a high metabolism. However, in terms of strength, you could have commented on another physiological concept – muscle fibres.

Muscle cells are long and contain two particular proteins – actin and myosin, which contract an active process (requiring ATP, and triggered by calcium ion release) to shorten and produce a force by pulling on the bones of the body via the ligaments. Therefore, the force produced may be related to either the number of muscle fibres (which macroscopically is the *size* of the muscle) or the density of muscle fibres. This is why The Incredible Hulk also has incredible bulk.

However, how might we account for superheros who are super strong but with a normal muscle bulk, eg Superman or Spider-man? The end result is still the ability to generate large forces, and so some possible mechanism including having different contractile proteins within the muscles which are more capable of generating forces than actin and myosin. They could be alien in origin in Superman, or produced by Spider-man's own body after his spider bite (possibly via a *virus* which caused a mutation in the DNA coding for the contractile proteins, leading to an abnormal, high-strength contraction mechanism).

(Note some of the language here – using terms like a 'quantitative increase to normal strength' gives a scientific appeal to the writing.)

Also, if you wanted to investigate more deeply, you could say that whilst big muscles create larger forces, giving rise to greater strength, they also require more energy and produce more waste products such as lactic acid and carbon dioxide. Therefore, our superhero might need to have a method to clear these waste products, such as an excellent blood supply and respiratory function.

Para 2

However, if we look at a super power which isn't an enhancement of a human feature, then we can look at flight. As we do not possess anything that resembles flight, we can look at other creatures which do fly. As I look at birds, bats, flying squirrels and flying fish I see that they all have a large surface area in order to support the weight of the flying body. So, to keep as close to a human body as possible, the bones could be very light by being hollow in the middle like a bird's and, like a flying squirrel and a flying fish, there would be a large flap of skin between the torso and the arms to allow flight to occur, as the large surface area would make it possible for gliding and so catching air currents.

You have started well by stating that flight is not a normal human feature, and we can look at other sources for possibilities. You have gone to a biological mechanism, which is to look at the function of birds, which I quite like. You list some of the key features which would enable a human to fly in a similar way, such as hollow bones, which again I like.

This is a difficult example to explain, but use it as an example to both show off your current knowledge and extrapolate it. You can delve into other realms of knowledge including Physics. In this case, a flying human gains both gravitational potential energy and kinetic energy by flying. According to the law of the conservation of energy (ie energy cannot be created or destroyed, only converted from one form to another), this energy must come from a source, and this must be inside the superhero. Therefore we can speculate that it must be stored as a form that is higher in density than our current highest-density tissue (fat).

How might it manifest itself? Well, we might be able to use the Bernoulli effect (movement of objects towards an area of lower pressure) to create lift. What we would need to do is draw a high-velocity draft of air over an asymmetric surface (eg as a jet engine does for a plane's wing) – could this be achieved through some kind of abnormal breathing (high velocity)?

Another theory is that we could use displacement in order to fly – which is to say that if we had a very low-weight body, the effect of gravity would be relatively lower, and therefore we could move around by displacing the air molecules around us, again via breathing. This is similar to low-gravity walking on the moon.

Para 3

Yet some superpowers will not be possible in the real world, such as telekineticity – being able to move objects with just the mind. This is because there has been no link at all between moving objects directly by just thinking that you want to move them.

I think this is a good caveat – this essay calls for scientifically sound speculation, and there are some powers which cannot be explained even with the best of current scientific reasoning.

Para 4

Another superpower that can't be explained is the ability to spontaneously freeze objects as even if we had an area of the body that was below zero degrees centigrade, then we would need a long time in order to be able to freeze an object.

This is an interesting power; what you have discussed is freezing via direct conduction, eg touching an object with a cold part of your body. However, I might speculate that there is moisture present in the air, and in order to freeze it you need to reduce the temperature, which is the vibration energy within the molecules. What will need to happen is an endothermic reaction, which requires the input of energy to occur. Examples include citric acid and sodium bicarbonate:

$$H_3C_6H_5O_7(aq) + 3\ NaHCO_3(s) \rightarrow 3\ CO_2(g) + 3\ H_2O(l) + NaC_6H_5O_7(aq)$$

Thus, the superhero might not need to be super cold; he might be able to produce two different substances in his body that could mix together and cause an endothermic reaction. This would be a reaction which takes in heat energy for its completion, leaving the surrounding area cooler.

Conclusion

To conclude, I do not think that superhumans with super powers will ever be able to exist in the real world despite some people arguing that it could happen due to a mutation in the genetic code and then, from natural selection, that gene will become prevalent in the population, so allowing more chances for a superhero to be made. However, natural selection doesn't really happen any more due to humans having manipulated the environment to suit them, so there is hardly any difference between an advantageous phenotype and a disadvantageous phenotype, if it is anatomical or physiological. The only phenotype that will be advantageous is one that makes someone much cleverer than others as now we live in an age where humans excel in brain, not physical strength. Also, if that gene becomes prevalent in the population, then the 'super powers' will no longer be super.

I think you have concluded very well for the most part, although I think you could strike a more balanced point by saying that you think it is very unlikely that superpowers will manifest themselves in real life – the old adage of 'Never say never' is certainly a good one as it is difficult to defend as a position. Don't forget that some superheroes do not have endogenous powers, but have an exogenous source for their power (eg Iron Man has an exoskeleton, Batman has the Batmobile), so technological advancement might make these possible as a military eventuality.

I really like the distribution/genetic argument you have made about super powers being non-super if they are widespread, and that is a very strong conclusion.

Overall I think you did well with a tough essay, but there were a few things which I think you could consider:

● Especially for Oxbridge submitted essays, if you can, use a wide range of examples from different subjects. As you have seen, including Physics and Chemistry as well as Biology will make you stand out amongst most potential Natural Sciences students.

- Use scientific terminology (endogenous, exogenous, quantitative, quoting laws of conservation, motion or endothermic reactions) to underline your understanding of the processes.

- Don't be afraid to think outside the box. Things like alien contractile proteins sound very unusual, but in the context of a good understanding of human physiology and a possible source of an alternate mechanism, it begins to be more reasoned.

Summary

- Essays are vital both in subjects where a sample is required and in aptitude tests.

- However, the principles of essay writing should be understood by *every* Oxbridge applicant.

- The characteristics which you must demonstrate are *organization*, *depth*, *breadth and innovation* and *critical appraisal*.

- For aptitude tests, prepare some examples which may be applied in multiple situations to give yourself the best chance of their being useful.

- For submitted essays, you have more time to do research to look for your examples with the title to hand.

- For any practice essay writing, you must actively seek feedback; this is the best way to learn.

CHAPTER 10

Special examinations

- Why are aptitude tests so important?
- How to prepare
- Universities, subjects and tests

Special examinations play an increasingly important role in your chances of selection to Oxbridge, and therefore you should pay an appropriate amount of attention to them. Many students are told that they 'cannot prepare for these tests'; this advice is, frankly, incorrect, and this chapter gives you the tools to give the best performance in these vital examinations. It is important to note that the essay section is a *very* significant part of aptitude tests, and this has been covered in Chapter 9.

There are a number of subjects which require a specific test as part of your Oxbridge application. This chapter details why these are so vitally important to your success, and the general principles of preparation. Pay particular attention to the format details and tips to give yourself the best chance.

Why are aptitude tests so important?

The academic aspect of Oxbridge applications is always the subject of controversy, as independent schools often take a large proportion of the top grades at A level and

GCSE. This means that the chance of entry to Oxbridge would be lower for state-school students if these exam results alone formed the selection process. The interview process is designed to mitigate this effect, but in recent years there has been a move toward aptitude tests as another fair and equitable arena for competition between applicants.

The research basis for the aptitude tests is very strong, and studies have shown that these tests are a strong positive predictor of success in university. There is a good correlation between high performance at such tests and high grades in the university examinations.

This research absolutely underlines the importance of getting these tests right, and unfortunately you only have one chance. It is therefore imperative to prepare as well as you can. However, it is not all bad news, as you may well find that a thorough revision programme for these tests also helps to build the foundations of your knowledge base for interview.

The difficulty is that these tests are designed to be less straightforward to prepare for. If you approach them as you would your normal examinations, you may be in for a surprise. This chapter will demonstrate how to maximize your performance both in terms of technique and on the day itself.

A warning for all students who have thought at some point during their preparation 'I'll just cram for it' or 'I'm fine in these kind of tests': if you are thinking this way, you are underestimating the extreme difficulty and significance of these special examinations. Almost all Oxbridge applicants will be good at taking normal examinations such as GCSE and AS levels, and in fact many of you will have found these relatively easy. However, these examinations are designed to address you as a group, and differentiate you into the best and the rest.

Therefore, anyone who is feeling particularly confident at this stage, please reconsider your position and work hard to give yourself the maximum chance of success. Don't let an attitude of arrogance become your downfall at this particular hurdle.

General advice

It is beyond the scope of this book to cover in great depth the knowledge required for each and every one of these papers. This knowledge, however, is not the key part of the examinations, and it is how to apply this knowledge in an exam setting that is so vital in aptitude tests. There are a number of important principles to bear in mind, as set out below.

How to prepare

Clear your schedule

It is important that you treat your aptitude test more seriously than your public examinations, as they represent the most important indicator for academic performance to the admissions tutors. For those of you who have not performed exceptionally well in your examinations thus far, it is a chance to redeem yourself in an environment which is not as dependent on your type of school. Even if you are a top performer in public examinations, a poor score can seriously harm your chances of success, as many students discover too late.

The next point is the timing of these examinations. Unlike your other examinations, which tend to be in the summer, and may be after an Easter break and revision breaks, these exams will occur in the midst of a busy term. Your final year at school is a busy time, and you will already have your UCAS personal statement and interview practice to contend with.

Furthermore, you will be progressing to A2 level, which means that free periods will become scarce and the workload will increase significantly. You may find that the subjects covered at school become more demanding. Preparing for aptitude tests is not as simple as public examinations. There is no easily accessible syllabus and a relatively limited supply of past or example papers. Therefore, you will have to work intelligently to increase your performance.

The following are some strategies for coping with yet another burden for your application.

Set aside specific time slots to undertake each of your Oxbridge application tasks

You may find you have a lot on your plate before you even started to consider the aptitude tests. In particular, writing the personal statement can sometimes feel like a black hole of time, where you can spend endless hours staring at the screen and willing it into brilliance. Try to set aside periods of 30 minutes or one hour, and after that time leave it for a while before coming back to it.

Similarly, try not to let the additional reading get out of hand at this stage. Allocate slots of one hour to read some material, and remember to utilize some of this time to write down a brief summary and some reflections or thoughts on the subject. This is vital to improving efficiency; you do not want to have to reread the material in order to understand it once again.

Last, manage your schoolwork efficiently. Try not to be a perfectionist when it comes to assignments, and give it a good effort whilst making sure you are not allowing it to steal too much time and energy from your application efforts. Focus on understanding the principles rather than spending an age looking up facts that you will forget by next week.

Your teachers may be more understanding about aptitude tests than about, for example, UCAS personal statements. This is because they are examinations, after all, unlike a piece of writing which you could have prepared earlier, and performance on the day itself is key. Therefore, talk to your teachers if you feel you are struggling with their work in the week or two before the exam, and they may give you some extensions on homework which can give you a breathing space to concentrate on the task immediately at hand.

All of these things can be prepared for in advance over the summer. In particular, try not to let your work on the personal statement be neglected over this period; if you have a framework or sample personal statement, this forms a basis for you to receive feedback on change and mould it. Make sure you have something to work with by the time you get back to school in September and it will take the pressure off your other activities.

Create a timetable

This will give you an opportunity to quantify what you want to cover and when it should be done. As you come towards the exam, you can allocate more time to its preparation, whereas the week before the UCAS deadline you may wish to focus on your personal statement.

Team up

Work with colleagues on preparing for your aptitude examinations. In addition to the general benefits of working together described in Chapter 6, you can gain benefit from sharing resources to save time and money. In addition, it can be helpful to explore the answers which your colleagues have come up with to see areas which you may have overlooked, and also to see where your suggestions are particularly strong.

Looking at format

Familiarity with the question type is one of the most reliable ways to improve your performance, particularly early on in your preparation. It is important not only to understand the format but also to practise answering so that you can focus purely on the content and not worry about the manner in which the question is posed.

Performance

Aptitude tests can often be time pressured and test speed and clarity of thinking. Make sure that you are well relaxed the night before the exam, and have a good night's sleep. Try to establish what makes you feel sharp and what gives the opposite effect. Try to avoid high doses of caffeine before examinations; this can make you feel more alert but it can also give people tremors and heightened anxiety as well as the unwanted side effect of more frequent bathroom visits. It is not a substitute for high-quality rest before your examination.

Have a clear plan of question timing in your mind. This will ensure that you spend an appropriate amount of time on each section. Bring a watch to facilitate monitoring time more easily.

Remember the rule of diminishing returns: you may spend too much time answering one question wonderfully and not gain the relatively easier marks of answering subsequent questions up to a good standard. Maintaining an even distribution of time throughout the exam gives the best chance for success.

Utilize online and published material to the maximum

You may find it helpful to utilize other sources of questions and answers apart from the main examination website. However, be cautious: it is difficult to say that all books will be helpful or value for money. Try to read reviews and spend time in bookstores looking at your potential purchases. Ask yourself the following questions:

- Are the question types actually similar to the style *and level of difficulty* which will present itself in my actual examination?

- Take a good look at the feedback. Does it explain the answers in a thorough way which adds value to your knowledge?

- Look at practical elements of the resource. Is it easy or difficult to flip backwards and forwards to the answers? Some aptitude test books have a poor layout which takes too much time to access the feedback and mark your own work, which is a cost you cannot afford, particularly at this critical period in the application process.

Universities, subjects and tests

Cambridge

BMAT (Biomedical Admissions Test)

This three-part examination for medical students comprises:

Section 1: Aptitude (60 minutes). This tests verbal and non-verbal reasoning and data interpretation in 35 multiple-choice questions.

Section 2: Science knowledge (30 minutes). This tests Mathematics, Physics, Chemistry and Biology at GCSE level of knowledge, but in more complicated *applications and situations*. It consists of 27 multiple-choice questions.

Section 3: Essay writing (30 minutes). Choose one essay from a choice of four, with limited space to complete a discussion of complex ethical, philosophical or scientific questions.

LNAT (Law National Aptitude Test)

A test for law students which involves:

Section 1 (95 minutes). Multiple-choice questions based on short passages which have a number of questions for each.

Section 2 (40 minutes). Choose one essay from a choice of around four. You will be expected to complete a balanced and well-reasoned argument for and against the point before coming to a conclusion.

UKCAT

A multi-section psychometric examination for medical students, comprising:

Section 1: Verbal reasoning (22 minutes). Reading passages and answering interpretative questions.

Section 2: Quantitative reasoning (23 minutes). Consists of 36 multiple-choice questions on mathematics, data interpretation and numeracy skills.

Section 3: Abstract reasoning (16 minutes). Consists of 13 questions which require you to identify patterns in groups of shapes. Students often find this the most difficult (and unusual format) – so practise, practise, practise!

Section 4: Decision analysis (23 minutes). Students must use a coding system to decode and encode sentences, testing their interpretation and grammatical skills.

Section 5: Non-cognitive analysis (30 minutes). Multiple-choice questions on ethical and situational dilemmas.

Oxford

ELAT (English Language Admissions Test)

A test for students of English to demonstrate their ability with unseen texts. The student has 90 minutes to analyse two texts, which can be prose or poetry, in a discursive essay, comparing and contrasting them.

TSA (Thinking Skills Assessments)

A combination multiple-choice and essay-writing skills examination which is used for a number of different subjects including Politics, Philosophy and Economics (PPE), Experimental Psychology, Economics and Management, and Psychology and Philosophy:

Paper 1: MCQ (90 minutes). Consists of 50 questions testing a variety of verbal reasoning and quantitative reasoning skills.

Paper 2: Essay writing (30 minutes). Choose one essay from a selection of three; essays have a rather open format and can be approached in a number of different ways; the student is expected to show excellent organization and example choices.

Linguistic aptitude test for Oriental Studies or Modern Languages

This test explores the understanding of the fundamental grammatical and comprehension rules of the language. There is one 30-minute short-answer paper.

Linguistic aptitude test for Classics

This test is different from the aptitude test for other languages, and lasts one hour:

Part 1 explores basic grammatical knowledge;

Part 2 requires translation and composition;

Part 3 looks at literary analysis and interpretation of a passage.

Mathematics aptitude test

A challenging examination of your mathematical ability:

Section 1: Multiple choice (40 per cent). Consists of 10 challenging questions with four possible answers.

Section 2: Long questions (60 per cent). A choice of four questions out of six, with marks given for showing working out.

Physics aptitude test

A two-part exploration of your ability in Physics:

Section A: Mathematical physics (1 hour). Consists of 11 numerically based physics problems.

Section B: Physics. A mixed section consisting of multiple choice, short answers and a longer, multi-section answer.

History aptitude test

A two-section examination based on historical text analysis:

Question 1 (1 hour). This is a multi-part question asking you to analyse a historical text before expressing your own ideas in the later sections.

Question 2 (1 hour). Interpretation of a piece of historical writing.

Summary

- Aptitude tests are critically important in representing your academic ability.

- They can and must be well prepared for.

- The majority of them have an essay component; refer to Chapter 9 for details of how to go about creating excellent Oxbridge-quality essays.

- Clear your schedule and create a revision timetable.

- Discuss with your teachers about having homework extensions in the period running up to your tests.

- Find as many practice papers as possible.

- Use online resources to supplement this material.

- Become familiar with the format of the examination to gain extra performance marks.

Further reading

For help with aptitude tests we recommend the following books, all published by Kogan Page:

How to Master the BMAT by Chris Tyreman;

How to Master the UKCAT by Mike Bryon, Chris Tyreman and Jim Clayden;

How to Pass Numeracy Tests by Harry Tolley and Ken Thomas;

How to Pass Advanced Numeracy Tests by Mike Bryon.

CHAPTER 11

What to expect from your Oxbridge interview

- Unpicking the mythical nature of Oxbridge interviews
- The interviewer's perspective: how do they construct questions and assess the answers?
- Interview technique
- Logistics: planning your journey, what to wear, what to bring

This chapter needs no introduction. Once all your hard work on the paper application has earned you a call to interview, you must prepare meticulously for this final and most difficult stage of selection. There are no hiding places, and no long periods where you can fine-tune and polish a personal statement or essay. You will be under the spotlight, and there are many dimensions to work on to give the admissions tutors the impression of a capable, interested, intellectually unsatisfied young student who will benefit from an Oxbridge application.

Unpicking the mythical nature of Oxbridge interviews

Oxbridge interviews are often surrounded by a mystique which consists of half-truths and misconceptions as well as reality. Here are some of the most common student and parent concerns, and the truth behind them.

Common pitfalls and myths

The questions are so unusual, it is impossible to prepare for them

This is the most common and horrific misconception. You must not get caught up in this mindset which may affect some of your peer group, or even teachers and parents. There are absolutely dozens of ways to help you prepare for a difficult interview, and in my experience the only thing holding you back from completing all of them is lack of time. This book details the obvious methods such as subject topics and practice questions. However, it also deals with more subtle and finer details such as language, non-verbal communication, panel management, cadence, identifying and responding to specific question types and many more. Take each and every opportunity to rise above the level of your peer group.

Oxbridge interviews are exceptionally difficult

This is true. They are designed to be conducted at a very high level, so that it becomes easy to distinguish the best students from a group of very good students. Remember that if it is difficult for you, it will be difficult for everyone, and do not become disheartened by not being able to answer some questions. In fact, interviewers are relying on this fact (see 'The interviewer's perspective', below). The most important thing is to show how you are thinking, and your interviewer will give you clues if you make an informed and intelligent attempt to answer.

Independent-school students will perform better than comprehensive-school students

This myth is patently untrue, and in fact, both Oxford and Cambridge are dedicated to equality of education for all students, and they are looking for the very top potential students. Lack of resources and poor teaching at a school will be much less of a hurdle at this stage, as most of the additional preparation I will describe does not rely on school teaching. Keen students from either the public or private sector will be able to compete in terms of the effort they put into preparation.

The interviewer's perspective: how do they construct questions and assess the answers?

Of all the topics I have discussed with admissions tutors, the interview is the one which holds the most interest for each and every one of them. This may reflect the weight of importance they put on it in the process in terms of selection; but it also reflects which element they enjoy the most.

One admissions tutor said: 'We teach in supervisions (one-to-two, small-group teaching) here at Cambridge; I am looking for students who will thrive in this environment. Teachers often gain as much out of the relationship as the students, and it is rewarding to discuss ideas and concepts with bright and eager minds. It is this characteristic which I search for during interviews.'

What insight does this give us? Dull, if informative, answers might not give this admissions tutor what he is looking for. Challenge yourself to be interesting and perhaps give the interviewer something they have not heard a dozen times already today.

How can you do this? You will need to demonstrate an excellent baseline level of knowledge. This cannot be avoided and does not necessarily make your answer boring or common. However, you can push the boundaries by introducing a unique structure into your response, or referring to interesting, novel or controversial work. All of the tools in this chapter and Chapter 12, which looks at specific questions and answers, are aimed towards achieving this goal as well as demonstrating your intellect.

The second insight that tutors have given me is that although the content of questions varies immensely, there are some common characteristics, thinking patterns or behaviours which they are looking for when designing the questions and listening to the answers. This has allowed me to frame the questions into certain groups based on the *type of answer* they are looking for. These can be described as:

- guesstimate type;

- description/explanation type;

- experimental design type.

As these are best covered by specific examples, they will be discussed at great length in the next chapter.

The bottom line is to try and put yourself in the shoes of the interviewer: how would you go about differentiating between students if you were them? Spending some time from this perspective can help you to shape your preparation, as well as take some of the fear and mystery out of this process.

Interview technique

- continuous chain (C-chain) questions;

- antagonistic chain (A-chain) questions;

- P-stops;

- body language;

- thinking pauses;

- panel management;

- cadence;

- written and diagrammatic elements of interviews.

The vast majority of your preparation for interview should not be based on technique – it should be focused on high-quality study, contemplation and understanding of your subject. However, as the interview approaches, being aware of how it works and some specific techniques to look out for can greatly increase the performance of a candidate who has and maintains a high level of knowledge. There is a vast amount of work you can perform in technical preparation – make sure that you practise. Employ practice with mock interviews with teachers if you can persuade one, and also with friends, family or whomever is willing to help you. Video recording your own performance will allow you to perform self-assessment on all of these technique areas and slowly improve your interviewing skills.

Each one of the following interview techniques has its own specific indication and techniques; consider them as individual issues to be practised in turn.

Continuous chain questions

Much of your interview will be continuous chain or C-chain questioning, which involves linking in questions based on your answers, what you have demonstrated so far and what the interviewer wishes to see more of. The extent to which this occurs will depend on the question type; but essentially a C-chain of interview questions can be considered 'normal' practice; it is therefore important to understand this because it differs from other types of interview progression, and this knowledge will allow you to differentiate between them.

Antagonistic chain questions

A question chain starting with a relatively neutral question may take a turn down a more confrontational route, which is known as an antagonistic chain or A-chain questioning.

This is a particularly common pattern of questioning behaviour which Oxbridge students may face, and is best understood by looking at examples. Consider these questions which were recently posed to Oxbridge medical applicants:

Candidate: I want to study medicine because I want to help people in a direct manner.

Interviewer: If you want to really help people in a hands-on way, why don't you become a nurse?

Candidate: I really want to work for an international aid organization such as MSF.

Interviewer: I see, and do you think the government should fund the training for doctors who want to go off and work in foreign countries?

The value of A-chain questioning centres around the interviewer challenging the interviewee by directly opposing their point of view, and seeing how they respond. Unlike the P-stop (described later in this chapter), an A-chain is more of a diagnostic tool and will commonly feature in the interviews of candidates who are performing well. In using A-chains, admissions tutors are looking for the following qualities:

● performance under pressure;

● reasoned argument;

● ability to maintain emotional distance from responses;

● ability to assimilate new information and learn from it.

Navigating an A-chain

Your goal is to demonstrate to the interviewer the qualities listed above. Therefore, poor responses are fast, unipolar and defensive answers. The best answers demonstrate all of the abilities which the interviewer is looking for. You can use the following five-step framework to terminate an A-chain and bring the questioning back to C-chains:

1 taking a little time to think;

2 acknowledgement;

3 arguments for;

4 arguments against;

5 balanced conclusion.

Taking a little time to think

It is important to take a little extra time to consider an A-chain response, more so than other questions. This is because, first, you will probably need the time to balance both sides of the argument. Second, if you are a candidate who has a tendency to rush out answers, this will look especially bad in A-chain responses as the interviewers are looking for reasoned answers rather than knowledge recall. Finally, there is a non-verbal communication element to taking a little time to think. Show the examiner that you recognize the complexity of the issue, which is then built on verbally in the next step.

Acknowledgement

Acknowledge the interviewer's position. Interviewers are looking to see if you are aware that their statement is controversial. Demonstrate your awareness of the complexity of the problem they are proposing. Using the first example above:

Actually, now that you mention it, nursing has quite a lot of similarities with what I would like to achieve.

Arguments for and against

Advance arguments for both sides, in a neutral manner. Use phrases such as 'some people believe', 'on the one hand'. Present the arguments in the third person rather than expressing what you think, eg 'Euthanasia can be considered a good thing if it eases the suffering of patients' rather than 'I think euthanasia helps to ease the suffering of patients.'

Again using our example:

Nursing involves the day-to-day care of patients, distribution of medications, dressing of wounds and countless other essential tasks in maintaining the healthcare of patients. Contrary to popular belief, nursing education does involve significant scientific learning and understanding in certain subject areas.

However, medicine approaches this in a different way, and uses a firm core of biological sciences, including disciplines such as pharmacology and pathology, to look at a patient and determine what is wrong with them. This has great intellectual appeal to those who, like me, enjoy using science to solve problems. The other important element is that doctors must also address the well-being of the patient, including their mental health, and this is undertaken by empathy and compassion.

Balanced conclusion

Use verbal triggers to indicate to the interviewers that you are concluding your argument. These are not catchphrases to score points but a signpost that you are reaching the end of your answer:

'on balance...'

'with these things in mind...'

'taking these into consideration...'

Associating value to arguments can help in demonstrating the intellectual process of balancing. For example, in answer to the nursing question, you could say that you value scientific interest and compassion equally, and therefore you are choosing medicine because it has a similar amount of compassion but more focus on science. This is a semi-quantitative balancing which demonstrates good reason. Simply saying 'on balance' does not necessarily show you have performed an analysis in this way.

Further worked example

Question: 'Why should we pick you rather than other better qualified candidates?'

Know yourself well. Remember that the primary selection criterion for Oxbridge is academic ability, and that is the easiest to 'quantify' by means of testing. However, the other qualities such as dedication, genuine interest, unsatisfied intellectual curiosity and initiative are less easy to quantify. Therefore you can approach the question in this way, and discuss these other areas which are important for future students. Be ready to defend your weaker areas, particularly if you got a poor grade in a certain area. It may not be helpful to make a whole load of excuses (retrospective analysis); rather, try to show what you have learned from these weaknesses and how your study patterns have changed (prospective analysis). This will allow admissions tutors to see how you learn from your mistakes. If you performed relatively poorly academically, be prepared with examples to demonstrate your ability and interest, which are outside examinations.

How to answer

I see the characteristics of an Oxbridge student and indeed all academics in the field of anthropology as needing academic ability, dedication, genuine passion, unsatisfied intellectual curiousity and initiative. Therefore I'm sure there will be candidates who are better qualified than me in some ways – but not all. I think I represent a rounded academic approach which is reflected in my choice of A levels, which balance Sciences and Humanities, and is complemented by my additional reading, which has had an in-depth look into Economics, Politics and Psychology to support my understanding of human behaviour. Even for those candidates who are better qualified than me on paper, I think there are some intangible qualities which I will bring to the course which are harder to measure, and the most significant of these is my interest and desire to study Anthropology.

How not to answer

A real answer in a mock interview:

Are you sure they are all better qualified than me?

- Have a sense of humour. This can help to mitigate over-seriousness. Make sure that your humour is appropriate and not coarse or offensive.
- Know your limits. It is much better to say that you don't know something than to be caught out not knowing something.
- Be friendly. An interview is really a conversation about yourself, and reflects how you might speak to academics or people in general.
- Be up to date on current affairs and have a considered opinion on them.
- An A-chain will be progressive and challenging. You will have the opportunity to defend your position and, if your defence is well considered and within reason, the A-chain will be terminated and questioning will move back to C-chains.

P-stops: pedantic comments or questions

Interview candidates have often been faced with the following kind of situation:

Candidate: I have always been interested in studying chemistry at university.
Interviewer: Always? So you've not really considered any other subjects?

Or:

Candidate: I was so tired I literally died.
Interviewer: I think you mean you figuratively died. If you literally died, you wouldn't be here.

These incidences of interruption of the narrative of the candidate with a mundane or unhelpful and non-progressive comment is known as a pedantic stop, or P-stop. It is a tool used by interviewers to correct the sense of a statement when the student has overreached themselves or said something without really thinking. When an interviewer finds a candidate loose with their grammar or making unsubstantiated comments, they will often indicate this by means of a P-stop.

However, it does not happen to all students. Why? This is because it is also a manifestation of dissatisfaction with the method of delivery of your answers. Candidates who make a minor overstatement whilst nervous at interview are often not corrected with P-stops; it is more the individual who feels comfortable with what they are saying but does not realize that the manner or degree in which they are saying it is wrong.

Notice how this is different from the A-chain. The interviewer is not encouraging you and putting some pressure on you. They are essentially expressing their annoyance. In short, it is bad news; the good news is, with practice you can prevent, and where necessary treat, P-stops and still come out on top.

Prevention

Ideally the management of P-stops is effective prophylaxis. Using grammatical structure with a degree of academic caution is the surest route to stopping this type of interaction. For example, rather than using words such as 'always' or 'definitely', consider softer options such as 'mostly' and 'commonly'. If you make a pronouncement such as 'Leaders always have good verbal communication skills', you might be given counter-examples proving you wrong, such as the silent leader who inspires by example. Introducing elements of humbleness in answers will also help to prevent P-stops. See the Tip box for further examples of how to avoid generating P-stops.

ACADEMICALLY CAUTIOUS CONSTRUCTS

You can use the following sentence fragments to help you:

- 'From what I have experienced so far...'

- 'I am beginning to learn about...'

- 'In the main...'

- 'The majority of cases...'

- 'This seems to involve...'

- 'The author may be trying to...' (as opposed to 'The author is using this to show us...')

- 'One possibility is that...'

- 'A method of doing this might be...'

It is important to see these tools for what they are. This is not a simple method of trickery to convince the admissions tutors that you are a good student. It is actually a genuine learning point: try not to see your academic world and subject in black and white. People who think in absolutes tend to not see all the possibilities – to their own detriment. Those who accept that there are often exceptions to the rules, and seek them out, tend to flourish.

Also, this does not mean you have to use this kind of academically cautious phrase in every sentence. There may be some principles or facts that you do hold as absolutes and cannot be expressed in such a cautious way. Nevertheless, it is always worth *questioning* the assumptions we hold; and when the admissions tutors see that you do it routinely, you will be one step closer to earning a place at their college and in their supervision or tutorial group.

Interviewers will be responsive to your performance. Several admissions tutors have mentioned that if a candidate has an interesting, balanced and intelligent narrative, they will often try to avoid interrupting. Conversely, they will have no hesitation in interrupting a student with poor structure, or who is loose with their language. This is not with malicious intent but it is an attempt to make them stop and think. Much as one might defibrillate a heart so that it restarts in a more rhythmic fashion, a P-stop is intended as a shock.

Acute management

If you do come across a P-stop, take it as an opportunity to have a pause and rethink the direction of your answer. First, verbally acknowledge the criticism, apologize and correct yourself. This is important in demonstrating how you deal with critical feedback, another characteristic which admissions tutors are looking for. This is because it shows you are teachable and will benefit from their expertise and wisdom.

Do not use phrases such as 'I meant to say...', which is retrospective correction and indicates some resistance to the criticism. Prospective statements such as 'I'm sorry, I should say...' indicate that you accept the error and look forward to correcting future practice, which is important both in grammar and your academic pursuits overall. For example, you might manage a P-stop in the following manner:

Candidate: I have always been interested in Chemistry at university.
Interviewer: Always? So you've not really considered other subjects?
Candidate: I'm sorry, I should say I have been interested in Chemistry for a long time. I suppose it seems a bit like 'always' by now, but really it started when I was choosing which GCSEs to take and I realized that the subject I most enjoyed was Chemistry. My mind was so captivated by the models of the atom and understanding their intricacies, and I wanted to read more on everyday chemistry such as how plastic was synthesized or the molecular structure of caffeine, to gain an understanding of how

small molecules have a huge impact on my own life. Once I started with simple experiments in the laboratory, my enthusiasm continued to grow and that led me to undertake a work experience placement with The Natural Soap Company to understand how they undertake their product synthesis and investigate new lines of products.

Minimize the time spent focused on this error by expanding your answer after the prospective correction.

A candidate who receives several P-stops but fails to respond appropriately is likely to score poorly, particularly in the areas of potential to be taught and communication skills.

A candidate who receives a P-stop, successfully navigates it and takes it as a cue to manage their language better will score well.

Ideally, through careful and intelligent expression and discussion of ideas, P-stops should be prevented and this will be one factor which reflects a high-scoring candidate.

Body language

Non-verbal elements have a key role to play in our general communication, but the first thing to say is that this is less so during Oxbridge interviews than other situations. For example, your body language can say a great deal about your subconscious, and a 'closed' body position (arms crossed, feet pointing away) can have a negative effect on social situations or when you are discussing feelings and emotions.

In contrast, the content of your Oxbridge interview will be intellectual debate. The ideal situation is that you should be able to communicate your ideas and arguments succinctly – so much so that you could be having your interview by telephone. In this particular setting, gestures, posture and tone of voice are less important than choice of words and the content of your answers.

However, apart from testing your intellect, admissions tutors will also be assessing your interest in the subject, and this is an arena where non-verbal communication will play a role. Being aware of all the non-verbal signals you are giving can make the difference between a talented student and a talented *and* passionate one.

As I have expressed throughout this book, the best way to culture a genuine response is to organically develop your interest. However, a well-prepared candidate may wish to ensure that they 'look' as enthusiastic as they 'feel', which is understandable. Here are some tips on how to achieve this:

● Undertake research on this topic. As with everything, look at people who are good at their topic: in this case, giving out informative answers in an enthusiastic manner. Even resources such as chat show hosts on daytime television can be useful to observe. Do they look interested in their guest? How are their bodies aligned, and how do they use expressions and gestures?

- Observe excellent teachers and lecturers – they make a living from talking wholeheartedly about their own discipline: something which you will seek to emulate. A fantastic source of free lectures is www.ted.com, which has a searchable engine for almost any topic. Other famous speakers in your field, or even generalists such as the late Steve Jobs of Apple can be surprisingly informative. You will make this learning process even more efficient by learning about your subject plus verbal and non-verbal communication skills all in one.

You can think about these various aspects of your body language:

- *Arm position*. What are you doing with your hands? Crossed hands may indicate defensiveness. Some people are comfortable raising their hands to their face when they are thinking, others are not. Try to achieve a balance of being able to use gestures and knowing when to keep your hands still to let your answers do the talking.

- *Body position*. Remember that you will be seated for your interview, so will not have too many options. Leaning forward to give your answers gives the impression of eagerness, and leaning back gives a contemplative air. However, try to do what feels natural for you and do not rock backwards and forwards at every opportunity, as it can become irritating.

- *Eye contact*. It is important to engage your interviewers. However, some students I have worked with take this too far, and give the impression of staring. You can break up your eye contact by, for example, looking away or to the side when you are thinking about your response. See the section on panel management, below, on how to distribute your eye contact effectively amongst multiple interviewers.

- *Legs*. It is best to avoid crossing your legs if possible as this will give a negative, disinterested air.

- *Facial expressions*. This will be the hardest to change and the key is not to try and overcompensate to demonstrate your 'thinking' face. There are a number of facial muscles involved in expression and deliberately controlling them will take away from your effort when you are actually trying to think.

- *Habits*. Do you have any particular behaviours which could be irritating to the admissions tutors? Do you drum your fingers, wring your hands, gesticulate wildly or tap your feet? Try to stop yourself from doing any of these or similar, ideally far in advance of the interview day itself. Ask your friends and family to mention these things when you are doing them in social or casual settings. Try to identify what your habits are by mock interviews, which can be enhanced further by making a video recording and watching yourself to pick out your faults. Remember the main aim is to keep the focus on your answers and not detract from this.

Overall, do not put too much emphasis on this area of preparation, but some carefully selected thinking and practice can really add some shine to a performance which is otherwise grounded in academic excellence.

Thinking pauses

Every one of my students appears nervous during their first practice interview. It would take a kind of logic-robot to avoid having the telltale signs of anxiety, in terms of voice and body. Most of these are not problematic – to the admissions tutor you may be the 10th or 15th student who looks this way on the interview day. It demonstrates that you are in fact human, and also that the interview is important to you. However, one of the elements of nervousness which can directly affect your performance is a phenomenon called 'reflex answering'.

Many students, *particularly when nervous*, will answer very quickly, sometimes before the final syllable of the question has left the interviewer's lips. This is highly negative for several reasons. First, it gives the interviewer the impression that they are not considering the question in full. Admissions tutors are not looking for how much knowledge you can recall; they are looking to push your boundaries and force you to construct answers to questions that you might in fact not necessarily know the answer to. Therefore, it is a bad indicator when the student appears to consistently use superficial thinking. Second, it is very irritating to the interviewer, and this is certain to impact negatively on their impression of you. Enthusiasm does not mean reflex answering. Last, it stops you from having time to plan out your answer, to reconsider or check its validity or to think about whether your answer is really aimed at addressing the question at hand.

As you can see, this type of answering is a technical flaw which must be avoided. Therefore, including a short thinking pause before your interview answers can avoid this problem. This means letting the interviewer *finish the question*, and then allowing *a brief period* for you to consolidate your thoughts in silence before going on to answer the question. There are several additional benefits from this strategy, which are detailed below.

Structure

The pause gives you a moment to gather your thoughts and in particular to think about a way to structure your answer. This involves what to prioritize and consider what is perhaps additional or supplementary information.

Active anxiety control

Giving yourself a little more time can help you to settle your nerves both mentally and physiologically before launching into your answer.

Quality control

Are you sure that the examples you have chosen are appropriate to illustrate the points or address the problem posed?

GETTING THE BALANCE OF PAUSING RIGHT

Practise introducing your thinking pause when you get the chance in mock interviews, or even in the classroom setting. This should last only a matter of a few seconds, and you will quickly learn how long you can pause before irritating your questioner! You will quickly learn that this is a battle between jumping in too early and overthinking whilst not communicating your thoughts to the panel. Use every chance you have with a mock-interview setting to fine-tune your pauses for the interview day.

Panel management

Oxbridge interviews will usually have two admissions tutors present; occasionally you may have one, or more than two. Therefore, it is important to understand some principles of how to manage this interview 'panel' in order to help the interview run more smoothly:

- Address your answer mainly to the interviewer who asks the question. In the main, you are addressing their question and engaging them in a conversation about the topic at hand. The remainder of the panel will 'overhear' your conversation as it goes on.

- However, take some opportunities to engage the other interviewers during your answer. It can be helpful to do this as you are changing point or section of your answer, as it underscores the *structure* of your answer, eg 'on the other hand...'. Look over and make eye contact, but after a short while remember to bring your focus back to the interviewer who asked the question.

- Always finish your answer when looking at the asker of the question. This will help to denote the end of your answer, in conjunction with other techniques in the section on cadence.

Cadence

This a method by which you can use the structure and tone of your reply to signal the end of an answer to achieve two main goals: maintaining a good *flow* to the interview and indicating the most interesting potential *follow-up* for the question. The first goal is of critical importance; after the interviewers' day full of stuttering, stop–start interviews with nervous students, if you can ease the transition from question to question it will help to make your session stand out. The second goal is a tool for you to direct more of the interview towards topics which you are more comfortable addressing; students who are well prepared can take full advantage of this.

Cadence is the design of tailored endings to your answers to achieve these aims. It involves selecting an element you want to focus on and introducing it as a lead part of your response.

Consider the following. In a multi-part answer, the follow-on question is most likely to be about the last answer, followed by the beginning answer, and least likely to be concerned with the middle. For example: 'My interest in Physics stems from a love of sciences and a genuine desire to study how the world is composed and how its matter interacts in various ways, which I have discovered more about through a number of exciting laboratory work-experience placements, including looking at the effects of laser and plasma in controlled situations leading to electron acceleration.'

Just as in physics, current flows down the path of least resistance, so an interviewer will usually follow the C-chain of most interest. The interviewer may well pick up on the cue of laboratory work experience and ask you about what you learned from that, or the area of interest, where the student may go on to discuss the work on the nature of ionized gases and their various applications, including spacecraft propulsion or more mundane usage such as televisions. However, it is important that you do not try to anticipate the next question. Rather, use the above techniques to help the conversation spend a majority of the time on subjects in which you feel more comfortable. In the example above, you should feel comfortable talking about the principles of physics in general, as well as your laboratory work.

Interviewers may want to explore areas which you have glossed over to see if you are hiding a gap in your knowledge or understanding, and thus will sometimes 'fight' your control of the interview by taking tangents that lead away from the general flow. Therefore it is important, when using cadence, that you are ready for questions that you are not expecting.

The other important aspect of cadence is the finishing of an answer in a manner that shows that it is in fact the end. Many inexperienced or nervous students fall into the trap of tailing off at this point, eg 'I think it could come under common law. Or there could be some legislature but I'm not aware of any particular statutes. Or...'

You will be surprised how often you leave the interviewer hanging on and waiting to see if there is any more information forthcoming, or whether they have to actively press you for it. The best way to avoid such problems is actually to stop using terms such as 'or' or 'maybe', and also to indicate with your tone and body language that you are expecting some further input from the interviewer. Some students incorporate a slight nod of the head in this procedure, as it gives an additional non-verbal cue to underline the transition further.

Written and diagrammatic elements of interviews

The majority of the advice given above deals solely with the verbal aspect of the assessment. Indeed, many Oxbridge interviews are conducted with nothing other than the materials retrieved from the minds of your admissions tutors and your own. However, many Oxbridge interviews contain an element of data interpretation, literary review or diagrams from the interviewer, or indeed require you to put pen to paper in some way.

There are some subjects in which this may be more frequent than others. For example, in Physiology you may be expected to look at simplified pen drawings sketched by your admissions tutor and infer principles and answers from it. In Economics you may well be expected to look at a sample of data to assess how well you critically appraise information in this form.

You can prepare specifically for this by practising useful techniques:

- For subjects where you may expect to draw something, you must spend some time practising basic outlines, which you can then have at your disposal in the interview setting.

- For Mathematics and Economics, you must be comfortable with the interchange between numbers, equations and graphs, particularly with inequalities and quadratic equations.

- For Physics students, can you represent particles quickly and efficiently to demonstrate principles?

- For Chemistry applicants, are you comfortable sketching organic chemistry formulae?

- For Biology students, you must be able to draw a basic cell, as well as all the major organ systems.

- Engineering and Architecture are more applied sciences and arts respectively, therefore you should be at least proficient at line drawings. Engineers should be comfortable with logic gates and simple sketches of such systems.

- Law students should have in mind a hierarchy of the British legal system, and historians may find Venn diagrams or spider diagrams helpful.

Supersize it

Generally speaking, large diagrams are easier for both parties to see and interpret than small scribbles, which are more akin to Chinese calligraphy than textbook drawings. Give yourself space to work in by increasing the size of your representations.

Leave margins

For drawings, try to focus your efforts on the centre of the paper you are given. This will allow you to expand on and add data or additional thoughts as you progress.

Deliver condensed information

A diagram is a great way to convey information and, more critically, to show your understanding.

Bring a pen and paper in your bag

If you really want to demonstrate something graphically, you can propose this to the interviewer: 'Actually, I think this is best represented in a graph/diagram – do you mind if show you what I mean?' They will almost always have a pen and paper on the desk; however, it can be useful to have your own. This method can demonstrate considerable intitiative and originality – but only if your diagram adds value to your answer. Do not draw all the time – it is important to show that you can communicate complex ideas verbally as well.

Finally, do not draw a complex diagram that takes too long. Interviewers will be impressed by your originality but will not wait an eternity for you to produce a diagram – 30 seconds to a minute should be your upper limit of testing their patience!

This book is probably the only place in the world where you will be advised that drawing neat circles can help you at interview.

My students who go to interview already have a simplified system of drawing the heart, a neuron, a nephron, the respiratory and alimentary system for biological sciences, and molecules, sound waves, a mass spectrometer, a television, a radio antenna and the suprastructure of the internet for physical sciences. Several of them have impressed their admissions tutors with their rapid and thoughtful illustrations and are now using their skills in Cambridge or Oxford tutorials and supervisions at a much higher (and more detailed) level. Practise your drawing *and* organization in a graphical way to follow in their footsteps!

Logistics: planning your journey, what to wear, what to bring

This section should be your checklist for the pre-interview period; there is a large amount of forward planning you must do to give yourself the best chance on the day.

Planning

When you get your letter inviting you to interview, the first thing you should do is have an evening off to celebrate. Congratulations. You have worked hard and convinced the admissions tutors that you deserve their time and effort to allow you to showcase your ability in the beautiful setting of Oxford or Cambridge. You will no doubt have had anxiety over this letter, and now is the time to let that all come out. Do something you enjoy, and reward yourself.

The very next day, however, the planning must begin. High-quality logistics planning is designed to:

- reduce your anxiety on the day itself;

- give you the tools you need in the week running up to interview;

- allow you to make the necessary purchases and travel arrangements;

- gain an advantage over your competition by using physiology and careful planning.

Logistics planning starts by making sure you will be able to arrive promptly in advance of when you are required to be there. This is because all other planning is useless if you are not in the right place at the right time.

First, identify if you wish to stay overnight at the university. This may be an advantage, particularly for morning interviews, as you will be able to wake up later and consequently could be fresher for the event itself.

However, be careful if you typically have difficulty sleeping in places away from home, such as in hotels and on holidays. If this is the case, look into the options for travelling on the morning.

Trains are a very popular way of travel and there are many options for most areas in the country.

Once you arrive at the destination train station, there may still be some considerable further steps in your journey.

Remember that your interview will be in the winter months and therefore you absolutely must prepare for inclement weather.

Arrive early and give yourself plenty of time for unexpected delays – allow time to have *at least one missed or cancelled train or bus*.

Bring some food with you!

I once received a text from a student of mine at 1 am on the morning of her Cambridge interview, saying she was a bit too nervous to sleep, and now she was hungry but didn't know what to do as she had nothing to eat.

Fortunately, I was able to contact a colleague (who is a notorious night owl and studies well into the small hours) to escort her to a well-known Cambridge establishment, the Gardinia restaurant on Rose Crescent, known and beloved to all Cambridge students as 'Gardies'. This is open until 4 am and serves countless nocturnal students. I asked my colleague to purchase her a chip butty with mayonnaise, as the high carbohydrate content would make her feel sleepier and hopefully settle her down.

She woke up to a college breakfast the next day and performed admirably at interview, earning a place to read Natural Sciences. However, as much as it is my aim to help each and every one of you, I will be unable to provide this service to most of my readers, as I need sleep to look after my patients and students! Therefore, please bring a supply of 'emergency' food in case of the midnight munchies, as they can have a severely negative impact on your sleep as well as mine.

Appearance

The dress code for interview is formal. For men this means:

- a suit in *conservative colours*;
- a shirt and tie that complement each other;
- tie done up to the collar (not slackly hanging down);
- *polished* shoes;
- tidy hair, as far as possible for your style.

For women it means:

- a suit or skirt suit in similarly conservative hues;
- moderate heels or flats;
- reasonable make-up – foundation, some blusher and mascara are fine; avoid bright lipstick or unusual eye shadow;
- modest accessories;
- avoid using perfume.

This is not specified dress code by all universities or colleges; however, I insist on this for my students for several critically important reasons. You must present your most mature, formal, committed and serious face on the day of the interview. A formal and smart dress code adds an important non-verbal element to this overall image. It shows respect for the admissions tutors who are taking the time and effort to assess you for the privilege of studying at one of the top institutions in the world. Your interviewers are likely to be senior academics who may have quite a traditional viewpoint on dress codes. It is not worth taking the risk of their frowning upon your chosen attire; play it safe, and no one will ever criticize you for looking smart and well presented.

You will hear of some students turning up in jeans, hoodies and the like, and I am certain some of your peers will choose to do so. That is fine for them, but do not be sucked into this attitude. Jeans and a T-shirt give the impression that you are stopping in for a quick interview on your way to the park or cinema.

A tidy and formal appearance helps the admissions tutors to extrapolate how you might choose to present yourself in the future. The additional benefits include not having distracting features such as unusual logos on your chest, or giant hoop earrings. Such things can draw attention away from the content of your answers.

Interview clothing dos and don'ts

- DO practise wearing your interview outfit, and feel comfortable standing, sitting and talking in it.

- DO bring a spare shirt. Drinking coffee or juice while nervous can cause unexpected problems.

- DO NOT wear casual clothing.

- DO NOT even consider wearing casual clothing.

What to bring

- Umbrella – you will be interviewed during winter months! A scarf, gloves and coat may also be necessary, depending on conditions.

- A printed map to your interview location – do not rely on your smartphone in case of any technological issues on the day!

- Written contact numbers for the college; this gives you a place to call in case of any problems. Go to the college website and find the number for the porter's lodge; if you call and explain you are a student coming for interview, they will be quite happy to help you.

- Spare cash – if possible bring £20, which should be enough for a cab to the most distant colleges in case you are running late.

- Several sheets of plain paper, pen and pencil.

- Emergency food – try to avoid spicy food.

- Entertainment – this is very important if you are staying overnight. You must have a way to unwind, whether it is a book, portable gaming device, music or anything you fancy.

If you have all these things ready in advance, you will be able to cope with many of the last-minute problems that could give you undue stress. This will allow you to fully focus on the intellectual challenge at hand, and give you another competitive edge over less-organized peers.

The night before the interview – things to avoid

Learning new material. There is a vast amount of material which you will have covered in your preparations up to this point, and the most useful thing you can do is to consolidate what you already know. Information will either be 'interview ready' or not; which is to say data that you know well, and more than just the bare bones. Moreover, it is important that you are comfortable verbalizing and discussing the material, and this comes about by a combination of input (reading, research) as well as practising output (mock interviews, practice with friends, talking about it in front of a mirror).

Any new information you acquire in the last couple of days will not be retained at such a high quality and therefore you should avoid wasting time on this fruitless activity. There may be some new developments, current affairs or new discoveries which you may come across. Nevertheless, it is the most common mistake for students to over-compensate for perceived under-preparation by doing lots of last-minute reading. This is highly counterproductive and will increase your stress whilst not having much appreciable positive impact on your performance. Build on your existing strengths at this time rather than trying to discover new ones.

Relaxation. It is very important that your mind is fresh and enthusiastic for the challenge ahead. Just as an actor who practises a scene too many times might find it hard to look surprised when a murderer appears from around the curtain for the 30th time, you might lose the will to discuss your love of your subject if it's been going through your head too often the night before the exam. You will therefore need an activity which can genuinely take your mind off things for a significant period.

Construct revision sheets to refresh yourself on key definitions and terms; also note down the anecdotes which you can draw upon for your subject, and extra-curricular questions.

Use physiology to your advantage. Experiment with your meals and find the type of food that you can eat *without* it making you feel sleepy – try to have the same or similar products available for the day of interview itself so that you will be able to give a fully energized performance under pressure. For many people, fat-rich foods such as fish and chips or burgers can cause bloating and make you feel tired. Sugary foods often give a 'high' as serum glucose levels peak but then give a rebound 'low' as increasing insulin levels drive the glucose into the cells, leaving you feeling shaky and weak. Avoid these quick-release snacks where possible, as many students have a tendency to have a chocolate bar around interview time to ease their nerves. A high-fibre alternative such as a banana may be better, or complex carbohydrates which take longer to digest, such as baked potatoes, wholegrain pasta or brown rice with meat and vegetables.

Caffeine can lead to an over-aroused state in which you appear more nervous, and may also heighten feelings of anxiety. Try to avoid taking caffeine on board unless you really have to; this is best done by having sufficient sleep!

All of the above are just guidelines, the bottom line being that people respond variably to different foods and it is important to establish your own personal optimal nutrition in the period before interview. You may also find these data useful around exam periods. Therefore, it is worth your time and effort to plan ahead and try out different possibilities to find the match of performance with taste to give a winning representation of yourself on the day.

On the morning of the interview

When you wake up, just remember that if you've been working through the exercises, questions and learning tasks in this book, you will be better prepared than most candidates. Be reassured that there are many people who think that they cannot prepare for interview, and you will be in a good position from all your hard work. Everything that you have been undertaking for these difficult months is behind you to support your efforts today.

The most important thing to bear in mind is what you are doing it for: a place in a wonderful university with all the opportunities you can imagine, and more. Today you will be speaking to world leaders in your field, and they will be pushing you to your limits. Revel in that experience, and really try to enjoy engaging with them in the mutual passion you share for your subject. If you keep this in mind, you will be in a good position to let your excitement and enthusiasm come to the fore, and improve your chances of success.

KEY POINTS

- Do some active relaxation to take your mind off the interview.
- Get a good night's sleep.
- Eat well and correctly.

Summary

- Students *can* certainly prepare for interview and there is a huge amount to do in this area.

- Always bear in mind what the interviewers are seeing in you when planning preparation.

- A-chain navigation forms an important part of your interview repertoire; practise it!

- P-stops are best avoided but can be cured.

- Cadence is a great tool for you to exert some control on the flow of the interview.

- Panel management requires getting used to talking to a group of people at the same time.

- You must spend some time on logistics to reduce anxiety and pressure on the day itself.

CHAPTER 12

Sample questions and answers

- General question advice
- The Specificity rule
- Sample general interview questions and answers
- Subject-specific advice
- Example questions and answers for Social and Physical Sciences
- Example questions and answers for Arts and Humanities

In this chapter you will learn to convince admissions tutors, and yourself, that you have the knowledge, understanding, commitment and desire to earn a place to study at Oxbridge. First, you must learn to cope with the general interview style of question, which looks at your motivation on why you wish to study at Oxbridge. Here, you will learn about the *Specificity rule* and how to apply it. You will then take an in-depth look at the three question types: *guesstimate, description/explanation* and *experimental design.* This is complemented by specific questions and worked examples for Social Sciences, Physical Sciences and the Arts and Humanities.

General question advice

You may have a general interview as part of your Oxbridge selection process; this will be very different from your subject-specific interview in several areas. First, it will be conducted by academics who may not be specialists in your field. The aims will differ too; they are to assess your general thinking processes and whether or not you have an 'Oxbridge' mind in the broadest sense of the term. They are likely to focus on questions on your motivation and commitment, and on points of interest from your personal statement. The interviewers may also ask some general questions about why you wish to study at Oxbridge and their particular college, which you must prepare for.

This interview is certainly important, and as such, you should review the general questions and answers below to help prepare for this particular hurdle. In addition, make sure you use the Specificity rule.

The Specificity rule

One of the tools for answering general Oxbridge questions is the so-called Specificity rule, which will help to give your answers more substantial bulk. Consider the following two student statements.

> Statement A: 'I am really looking forward to the tutorial system, and exposure to cutting-edge research in a prestigious institution such as Cambridge.'

Try to imagine this from the perspective of an interviewer. What questions might you ask yourself about this statement? Does this student understand what the tutorial system is, and will they benefit from it? This does not mean they have more than a superficial level of comprehension about what actually goes on in this institution, and what the benefits are.

The next part of the statement deals with cutting-edge research, another prime advantage of an Oxbridge education. What exactly are they referring to? Do they know what is going on at the cutting edge? What are the major categories? What areas in their field are well known, and which are less well known?

As you can see, what looks like a reasonable answer to most students actually gives rise to more questions in the mind of the interviewer, who may then go on to ask further testing questions; but the best students will help the flow of the interview by dealing with these questions. Now consider statement B.

> Statement B: 'I look forward to the tutorial system and I hope to engage in greater amounts of discussion as my understanding of the subject increases. I also look forward to participating in cutting-edge research; at the moment I understand there are several groups in the Mathematics department looking at developing quantum cryptography, which I find particularly interesting as it

addresses a genuine need for secure communication, using techniques only made available since the advent of quantum computation. However, I hope to discover new areas of interest as my course progresses.'

Notice how this student vastly improves on the first answer. She uses *specific, named* examples of research, giving some detail whilst leaving this topic as an obvious one for the tutor to explore. In reality, she had already undertaken significant research into the basic principles of quantum cryptography.

This student also has a *specific* element of the tutorial system which is named, and this helps the admissions tutor to address some of the concerns raised in answers similar to statement A. In addition, it prevents the tutor having to ask smaller further questions such as 'So what research in particular are you interested in?' and allows them to progress to much more substantial (and interesting) questions such as 'What are the current difficulties in developing a quantum cryptography system for transatlantic communication?'

Therefore, the Specificity rule states that inserting a named, specific example to back up your statements has the dual advantage of demonstrating your knowledge and understanding, whilst at the same time maintaining the flow of the interview. Therefore, you should do this wherever it is feasible in your interview.

Think about this rule and try to apply it to the following general questions in the next section, as you generate answers that are unique for you.

Where can you find up-to-date information on the research activities of the university?

The best way is to find it online, by looking at the departmental website for your subject. Often there will be a dedicated tab or page which is denoted 'Research' or 'Research interests'. This is clearly a good way to start. Another way is to find the biographies of the leading academics within the department. Within their biographies will be statements about the research interests of leading academics in the department. Finally, if this has not yielded any fruitful results, you can try to look for a page on the publications produced by the department. This is commonly entitled 'Publications' or 'Published work'. The downside of this final method is that this will represent work that has already been completed, the results obtained and the research written up. The upside is that it gives you an idea of the achievements of the department, and a feel for where it might be heading.

Wherever you finally find the information, do *not* simply write down what is there and regurgitate it during the interview. This is a pointless exercise which can be easily exposed by follow-up questioning. You should try to place it within the scheme of your own knowledge of the subject. For example, if the department has ongoing activity on the genetic code of particular algae with a view to optimizing biofuels, which areas of your current understanding may be linked to this?

First, gene sequencing is part of the study of genetics, which in turn is part of cellular biology and biochemistry. Biofuel efficiency is also part of biology in terms of ecology (and its impact on the environment), as well as physics and chemistry (energy and its relationship to breaking bonds). Therefore, you can start to think about how this branches out into your chosen subject. Think about what other biofuels you know, where they are being used and how efficient they are. Read about gene-sequencing techniques – what is the latest one being used? What are the general principles of how it works? Could you explain these fundamental principles at interview in a few sentences?

You can see how looking up current research is not a simple matter to be allocated a few minutes of your time. Treat this as an intellectual exercise to stimulate further revision, organization and creativity in your thinking about your chosen discipline. Some students feel they benefit from drawing a map of the sub-topics and placing pins or Post-it notes in the areas where the research applies. This can be very helpful in giving a visual overview of your subject (although it can use up a great deal of physical space!).

Sample general interview questions and answers

Why have you chosen Oxford/Cambridge?

This question is both immensely common and immensely broad. Do not be frightened by its scope; use it as an opportunity to start quickly out of the blocks and show all the characteristics we have discussed previously. This is one of the questions which you can prepare for, unlike some of the other more impromptu or unpredictable ones below; therefore take your time to design your answer. You can generally think of your answer in two main divisions; general Oxbridge advantages and subject-specific issues.

General Oxbridge advantages

Refer back to Chapter 1 for full details of the advantages that were described: tutorial system, academic resources, academic activities and graduate prospects are the main categories to focus on.

Follow the Specificity rule to try and go into more detail about some of the particular elements; for example: 'I am particularly attracted by the tutorial system here. I have had relatively little experience with this up until now, but when our teacher arranged small-group discussion before a school presentation, we did have a sit-down session with just the three presenters and the head of the Geography faculty. It was fantastic to be able to discuss my chosen topic, which was wealth inequality in emerging markets – particularly China – in such great depth, as well as being a wonderful learning experience. I feel that this level of teaching is a great privilege, which I will continue to earn with dedication and hard work.'

This type of answer allows you to be different from the other candidates, which is important: almost everyone will know in theory what the advantages of a tutorial system are; this method allows you to demonstrate reflection on your own learning as well as show why you might be suited to such an environment. It also uses a prospective finish, which is also humble in nature – certainly a good thing to start off with as admissions tutors rank arrogance as one of the absolute most negative characteristics which can come out as a student.

One of the other features is the collegiate system, which operates such that your education through lectures is delivered at the site of your main faculty but your small-group teaching takes place at your college, which also provides your accommodation and pastoral care. Sports, activities, social events and dining also occur within colleges.

Although there are many non-academic aspects which may appeal to you, remember to put a strong focus on the academic ones. This will allow you to show your interviewers that you are a serious student who places study at the top of their priority list. There is scope for alternative answers, including tradition, beautiful settings and extracurricular activities, but never forget the focus of the admissions tutors themselves, which is primarily to find and nurture the finest minds of the world; help them identify you as one of these targets.

Subject-specific issues

In the first instance, there may be some particular attributes in the Oxbridge course which you are unable to undertake at other universities, and this is a tempting area to start with. However, it is important not to make this the sole reason for your application; you do not want the tutors to feel that you were left with no choices, and only applied to Oxbridge because this particular subject or subject combination was available here. This is important, especially in subjects which are very Oxbridge specific, eg PPE at Oxford. The best way to avoid this is to expand on your original answer, to cover why you want to pursue this particular subject combination and then discuss the specifics of how Oxbridge teaching is different from that of other institutions.

You must demonstrate that you know about the Oxbridge course and the difference between it and other courses. The level of teaching is different, in that you will be given two-to-one small-group teaching, typically for each subject that you take; and that you will be given essays to write in almost all subjects. This particular trait is one that you may be able to comment on; for example, you may find that Literature students have complemented their subject choices with History, Politics or other strong essay-writing subjects; let the admissions tutors know how this has improved your written communication skills. On the other hand, within science subjects, laboratory exposure and a focus on experimental design and research are something that are common to all disciplines. This may once again be something you can refer back to in your own work, and it is a good opportunity to combine both your experiences in school with any extracurricular placements such as work experience postings with research groups.

Key features of Oxbridge:

- small-group teaching on a two-to-one basis;
- teaching and research;
- academic support facilities;
- some unique subject options such as PPE or PPS;
- the collegiate system;
- very wide choice of third-year subjects, including those that may not be directly related to your own.

In considering your answer to the question of why Oxbridge, think through the various advantages of the course. You may find it helpful to phrase these in a positive light, eg 'I am looking forward to in-depth study of the basic sciences underpinning Medicine, as an extension of my interest in school-level Biology and Chemistry' rather than 'I don't really like the sound of problem-based learning; it sounds rather fluffy, so I prefer Oxford.'

Additional segments can help to cement your approach; for example: 'Having spoken to several current students, I can see that they are particularly enthusiastic about laboratory research, both in terms of learning new techniques such as PCR, and undertaking meaningful research at the cutting edge of science. This prospect really excites me, and is one of the major reasons for my application.'

In this case, the student chooses to display not only their understanding but also the source of this information, which demonstrates that they have taken the time to get to know their course. It also maintains a tone of genuine excitement to finish with, which plays an important role: admissions tutors admit that whilst a few students seem to be able to simulate interest in a subject, the most convincing 'performances' are those by students with a bona fide passion for the subject. If the subject really excites you, try to represent your feelings in your answer.

Why this college?

In terms of selecting a college, think about the considerations you have when using the college selector, and then narrow down your shortlist from there. What were the particular points which stood out for you? As you will be interviewed by tutors from that college, try to be as complimentary as possible; after all, many of the academics live on site and eat at 'High table' (within the college dining hall, a table reserved for the staff, which is often separated from the student body), and they will be fond and proud of their setting.

Other considerations include whether or not you would prefer to be in a smaller college which has a more intimate or family-like social dynamic, and people get to know each other well, or a large college with the opportunity to meet many different people. You might be interested in specific activities which are strong in certain colleges, such as rowing or rugby, and again some research will reveal the answer. Don't forget that these points are important but they are seen as peripheral activities by admissions tutors, so make sure you demonstrate that you are there to study first and foremost. If you like the library, literary or cultural societies, this is the place to mention it, as it will surely benefit the academic impression that you give whilst still being in context for answering the question.

Why are you suited for Oxbridge?

First, it is important to identify those characteristics which would make you a good student for Oxbridge. Consider the following:

- academic ability;
- independent study;
- creativity and an explorative mind.

Try to synthesize an answer which addresses these important criteria in turn.

For example, one of the less common ways to lend weight to your response is to refer to a specific comparison group: current students. It demonstrates that you have taken the initiative to find out what Oxbridge life is really like from a reliable source. It also gives you a chance to give a prospective element to your answer. For example:

> I talked to many students, and one point in particular stood out. My school has
> a number of successful students, and many of them are very good at last-minute

cramming for exams. I take a far more regular and organized approach which has allowed me to do well whilst allowing me plenty of time to continue playing the piano and violin and playing lacrosse, all to a high level. Although I met a few crammers here too, the majority do take a very long-term, carefully planned approach to study. Therefore, I feel my study habits also make me a good candidate for Oxbridge, and in addition I feel they will continue to improve as I meet more like-minded people.

> You can use this opportunity to introduce some of the impressive additional academic activities you have undertaken. Think about your 'showcase' of achievements or activities. Which ones are unique and required the most initiative? These may well be the ones the admissions tutors are looking for; take this chance to prove to them that you can make the best use of the university course and their teaching. For example:
>
> Building on my A-level studies of Euripedes, I went on to write a comedy play, ironically entitled *Tragic tragedies*, which explained the principles of tragedy and gave humorous examples of when Hollywood films got it wrong, to comic effect.

How do you cope with stress?

This question often catches students out on an internal inconsistency, as follows. Consider the problem of stress. Usually it will occur when you have too many things to do and not enough time. Therefore, there is a real problem with this type of answer: 'If I'm stressed out, I like to relax with music and sports.' It does not address the root cause of your stress – rather it can actually compound it as you are taking time away from what you are meant to be doing, if this is the only approach you are taking.

Therefore, the more sophisticated way to deal with such a problem is to take a *compound* approach to things. First, *show your understanding* of the cause of stress, then come up with a *strategy* for dealing with this cause; and finally, understand the *psychological aspects* of it, which involves relaxation.

For example:

Stress is caused by the perception of having too much to do in too little time. Therefore, the best way is to plan ahead and avoid it by having an accurate assessment of how much you can cope with and not undertaking too much that is beyond your capacity. However, if it cannot be avoided, the best way is to use organization to your advantage. I divide the work into discrete tasks. It is easier to see progress and therefore keep myself motivated with achievement milestones. I also reward myself with some relaxation time after completing each task; this helps me to deal with the psychological impact of stress, and I find 10 minutes of listening to music in a quiet room, or talking and complaining to a friend, can really help me feel better and more productive.

> Parkinson's Law states that work expands or contracts to fill the time allocated for its completion; you can take advantage of this law by specifying time slots to finish work in. Don't forget that Parkinson's Law has elastic limits; therefore, if you allocate an impossible amount of time to do the work it will no longer apply.

Know your personal statement

For the general interview, you may find your admissions tutor dips into your personal statement to pick up on details and discuss them further with you. You should therefore think about the answers you might give, and how to express the details to maximize the impression of academic interest and excellence. They may also ask you 'What is the most interesting thing you have done?' or 'What is your greatest achievement?' In this case, you should try to refer to something in your personal statement *and elaborate on it*. This is because it would be unusual for you to have achieved something wonderful but not put it down in black and white; on the other hand, it would also be unhelpful simply to report back what they have already read. Use it as a springboard to capture their attention with a fascinating story about your activity, and remember to reflect on what you learned from this.

Subject-specific advice

This section is divided up into two gross categories:

Social and Physical Sciences. Social sciences: Philosophy, Architecture, Law, PPE (Politics, Philosophy and Economics – Oxford), PPS (Politics, Psychology and Sociology – Cambridge), Politics, Economics, Psychology, Archaeology and Anthropology. Physical sciences: Biology, Chemistry, Geography, Geology, Physics, Medicine, Mathematics, Plant Science, Computer Sciences, Biochemistry, Engineering, Pharmacology.

Arts and Humanities. History of Art, English Literature, Modern and Medieval Languages, Music, Classics, History.

Each section will give an overview, subject-specific advice, and then example questions divided by type as well as subject. It is designed in a way to give advice that is both useful for your subject itself and underlines the importance of inter-disciplinary knowledge to help you demonstrate the type of depth *and* breadth of knowledge which the interviewers are looking for.

There are some key differences in the way that each group will be tested. Furthermore, you will gain great insight into structures, tools and examples from looking at questions within your section, even in subjects which are not your own. These principles of great answers can be capitalized on for whatever comes your way.

Social and Physical Sciences

Overview

To assist you further, the following subjects have been placed into a group or 'axis' which has a number of interrelations – try to explore through your reading and discussion with subject teachers in particular what the important links are between the following subjects.

TABLE 12.1   Subject axis table

Socio-politico-historical axis	Logical-numerical-calculative axis	Biochemical axis
Geography	Geology	Chemistry
History	Physics	Biology
Politics	Mathematics	Plant sciences
Economics	Computer Sciences	Biochemistry
Anthropology	Engineering	Pharmacology
Psychology		Medicine***
Philosophy*		
Architecture**		
Law		
PPE		
PPS		
Land Economy		

*Philosophy has strong links to Mathematics, particularly in the area of Logic.

**Architecture does have some design elements which can benefit from Physics and Engineering.

***Medicine at Oxbridge requires proficiency in all the sciences, which will additionally include Physics and Mathematics skills for most students – these are tested in the BMAT exam as well as at interview.

General principles

For Physical Sciences disciplines, it is important that you gain a feel for the vast importance given to experimental pursuits in Oxbridge. The nature of cutting-edge research, whether it is in the high-energy environment of the Large Hadron Collider (LHC) or testing the effects of ginseng extracts on animal hearts in a physiology laboratory, is to pose a hypothesis and gather data to prove or disprove it.

Therefore, understanding historical 'landmark' experiments can help you produce excellent answers as well as cementing your own comprehension. These are well-known events which have helped to support important theories. For example, one past interview question was 'How do we know that the speed of light is 3×10^8 m/s^2?' You may find it difficult to answer this question without referring to the Michelson–Morley experiment, which was a failed experiment testing for a 'luminiferous ether' through which light was conducted, which is why it had a constant speed. Although this demonstrated a conducting medium, the consistency of the speed of light remained, and you can go on to describe the problems of one-way measurements of the speed of light and the subsequent successes with two-way measurement.

Further example

'Are humans still evolving?'
Example:

> We could test for variation if we conducted a 'census' of genomes and analysed the DNA of people in different generations, and looked for patterns which might emerge in terms of genotypes – are they converging or diverging? For cost efficiency, we could take a random sample of humans and see, over time, how the diversification of the genome was occurring, via gene sequencing. Fredrick Sanger at Cambridge developed one of the first rapid methods for sequencing by using modified nucleotides which cause termination of a DNA chain as it is being extended. Introducing them into replicating DNA gives rise to DNA fragments of different lengths, which can be separated by electrophoresis, giving rise to 'bands' in a gel medium. This can be read in four groups as A, T, G and C nucleotides, and the positions of the bands can be used to read the DNA sequence.

Knowledge of Sanger's experiment demonstrates to the admissions tutors that you have an understanding of the basic structure of DNA and an important discovery in modern biological sciences. Looking at the experiment you have described, you can see that interviewers may go on to ask you about the basis of electrophoresis, or how DNA replication occurs. Therefore, you should let the experiments guide your further reading into areas of interests.

Try to read widely on the various key ideas, techniques or experiments that form part of the history of your subject. Not only is this invaluable for interview situations, but as an aspiring future social or physical scientist, you should be interested in how our current body of knowledge has come about. One interesting method to read up on experiments is to refer to a list of Nobel Laureates in your field, and look up their work to see why it was considered so important. This is a vital source of information and, of course, covers many subjects including Social Sciences such as Economics. The evidence base for principles on Geography, Psychology, Anthropology and many other of the social sciences can also be thought of in terms of experiments and data.

What are the experimental equivalents for Law and Politics? These must be land-mark cases and times of political change and, again, being familiar with the most famous and historically significant events in your particular field will help elaborate your answers as well as show the dedication to your subject by your research. For both subjects, you may wish to focus first on the history of law and politics in the UK, and then develop comparisons to systems overseas.

Subject-specific advice

Unlike the Arts and Humanities section below, this section will *not* contain an individual worked example. This is because there is a huge section on this which follows, which is broken up into question types rather than question subjects, which is a better way to approach the problem of interview practice. It will help your understanding further not to look at those questions which are purely aimed at your subject; as we have discussed above, you can gain so much additional benefit from reading other subjects' questions and answers that I have designed the following section to make that activity compulsory.

Having said that, it can be helpful to consider very specific questions that may occur in each subject, and these are described below:

Archaeology and Anthropology

- 'What is anthropology?'
- 'What is your favourite ancient civilization, and why? In what ways is it superior and inferior to our civilization today?'
- 'Describe your circle of friends in anthropological terms.'
- 'Tell me about these primitive axes.'

Architecture

- 'What is the future of architecture?'
- 'Tell me about your favourite building. Who was its architect, and what is the relationship between the building, its function and location, and its architect?'

- 'How would you approach designing a building for inner-city children to experience arts and sports in?'

Economics

- 'Why might the poorest people in the country *not* benefit from a 50 per cent tax rate for the richest?'
- 'What approaches can we take to tackling wealth inequality in developing countries?'
- 'Using advertising as a model, tell me about the assumptions a company would have to make in order to plan their budget and spending on various forms of publicity.'
- 'What is a Black Swan event? Why can these be so important?'

Geography

- 'Which is more important, human or physical geography?'
- 'Tell me about some methods you are familiar with in the study of geography.'
- 'Does global warming exist? Why is there conflicting opinion on this phenomenon?'
- 'What is the relationship between feng shui and geography?'

Land Economy

- 'How does a country prioritize dealing with national poverty versus poverty overseas?'
- 'What are the problems with inner cities in the UK and how can we solve them?'

Law

- 'Looters during the 2011 London riots were given steep sentences for what would normally be considered minor crimes. What do you think of this? Do long sentences act as a deterrent to crime?'
- 'Why do certain crimes in some countries still carry the death sentence?'
- 'Women should not be allowed to serve on juries because they are more subject to hormonal influences in their behaviour than men. Do you agree?'
- 'How do cyber-crimes reflect real-world crimes, and in what ways do they differ?'

Philosophy

- 'If you knew that there were 10 better people than you for the 10 places to read Philosophy at our college, would you tell me or not?'
- 'What is philosophy?'
- 'Is aiming for happiness the best way to conduct our lives?'

  – 'Not making the study of philosophy compulsory in schools contributes to the decay of our society. Discuss.'

Politics

  – 'What is democracy?'

  – 'What is the role of a government? Give examples of governments which have not fulfilled their role.'

  – 'How can we incentivize politicians to truly make decisions that are to our benefit?'

  – 'Which is more fair, the current UK proportional representation, or the Alternative Voting system?'

Psychology

  – 'Are violent crimes instigated by violent video games?'

  – 'Are the causes of drug addiction and gambling addiction fundamentally the same?'

  – 'What role is your subconscious playing in this interview?'

Sociology

  – 'Explain the phenomenon of chavs in sociological terms.'

  – 'Is the UK still racist?'

  – 'Is the age of monogamy in decline?'

Theology and Religious Studies

  – 'I'm an atheist. How do you feel about my view on the world?'

  – 'What is the significance of study of reliability and consistency of ancient texts to our knowledge of theology?'

  – 'What principles are common to the various faiths around the world? What is the most significant way in which they differ?'

For combination subjects such as Politics, Philosophy and Economics (PPE), and Politics, Psychology and Sociology (PPS), you must look up questions under each of the relevant headings.

Biological and Biomedical Sciences (including Biochemistry)

  – 'Which gene would you want to modify in yourself, and why?'

  – 'Telomeres are the secret to eternal life. Discuss.'

  – 'Can you give me an example of an area in biology which is still not completely understood? If I gave you a million pounds, how would you go about researching it?'

– 'Can you explain what would happen if I scaffold stem cells to cardiac tissue in a living human?'

Chemistry/Chemical Engineering

– 'How are alchemy and chemistry related, and what can we learn from alchemists?'

– 'How would you go about explaining the atom to a 12-year-old?'

– 'What issues might there be if you wanted to create a metallic oxide which had good conductive properties but was also transparent?'

– 'If you were held captive by drug dealers and asked to make them something profitable, what would you try to make and what equipment would you ask for?'

Computer Sciences

– 'Can computers have a conscience?'

– 'What is the significance of multi-core processors for programmers?'

– 'How many megabytes of data are there in your head right now?'

– 'Explain the principles of encryption'

Engineering

– 'You mentioned you play football. Can you describe the forces on the ball at various points in the game that influence its motion?'

– 'What are the dangers of magnetic-levitation-based trains and how have they been overcome?'

– 'Describe the most complex structure in this room and relate that structure to its function.'

– 'If you were sent back to the Middle Ages, how could you make something fly using only their level of technology?'

Mathematics

– 'I arrange five apples and four oranges in a circle at random. What is the probability that the oranges will be in pairs next to each other but each pair is separated by at least one apple?'

– 'Prove that $1! + 2! + 3!$ ... does not have any square values when $n>3$.'

– 'Consider $X^2 + Y^2 = Z^2$. Can you prove that XYZ is a multiple of 60?'

– 'How can the study of mathematics influence art and philosophy?'

Medicine/Graduate Medicine

– 'Is medicine a science or an art?'

– 'What are the negative effects of anti-retroviral drugs?'

- 'What are the cellular mechanisms which give rise to MRSA?'
- 'What are the differences in physiology between sitting and rowing?'

For 193 additional questions, please refer to *Succeed in Your Medical School Interview* by Dr Christopher See, published by Kogan Page.

Veterinary Medicine
- 'What is the largest contrast in animal physiology to human physiology as far as you are concerned?'
- 'How does our treatment of poultry relate to outbreaks of Avian flu?'
- 'Why are you more interested in treating animals than humans?'

Physics
- 'If a clock is running 33 per cent slower than usual, what percentage of time will it display the correct time over a week?'
- 'What are the criticisms of the theory of relativity?'
- 'Why are there so many misconceptions surrounding the Large Hadron Collider?'
- 'What is the evidence supporting the Higgs boson particle?'

Example questions and answers for Social and Physical Sciences

Oxbridge interviews are surrounded by a mystique which has confounded and frightened students for years. The focus of the questions is almost entirely on testing your scientific knowledge, but more importantly your application of this knowledge to situations you will not be familiar or comfortable with. It therefore goes without saying that in preparation for your interview you should revise carefully your school materials and subjects in either social or physical science.

One of the main concerns that students have surrounds being asked very unusual questions to which you seemingly do not know the answers. This chapter will break down these most challenging questions by type, and allow you to develop the skills required to analyse the problem and utilize your existing body of knowledge to synthesize an answer, which will allow you not only to respond with fluency and skill, but also with a desire to seek out more. It will also give you the knowledge you will require to answer questions regarding the university itself, the course and your motivation to get into your college of choice.

There are three distinct types of questions which you might be faced with during your interview. The first type is the guesstimate type, which involves a puzzle to determine something which you have no way of being able to actually answer – for example, 'How many footballs can you fit into an aeroplane?' – and can be solved by using approximate and reasoned figures. The second type is the description/explanation type, such as 'Tell me about the alternative voting systems' and requires you to use your existing knowledge to figure out what might be going on in the question. The third and often most challenging type is the experimental design type, such as 'How would you weigh your own head?' and requires an excellent understanding of statistics, principles of experimental data and confounding factors, as well as the ability to think outside the box.

Arts and Humanities questions do not quite have the same categorical methods of assessing answers, and therefore cannot be studied in exactly the same way. However, students may still find many of the principles in this section useful. In particular, the use of structure, comparison and examples is a theme that will emerge time and time again in all forms of interview for any subject. However, please refer to the specific Arts, Literature and Linguistics section below for more specific advice.

Guesstimate questions

Guesstimate questions are those which involve a puzzle to determine something which you have no way of being able to actually answer; for example, 'How much water is there in a cow?' You certainly will not know this answer off the top of your head. Many perplexed students will be stunned for some time, and blurt out a random guess. Others will vent their frustration, saying 'How could I possibly know the answer to that?' However, the key to tackling such questions is to use them as an opportunity to show the interviewers your current level of knowledge, and use application and deduction to estimate an answer.

One important element of answering such questions is to materialize the unknown quantities as best you can. This method is demonstrated in the first question below.

How many footballs can you fit into an aeroplane? (Mathematics, Physics, Engineering)

This seems like a difficult question at first, but the knowledge which you will need for it is relatively basic. If you do not know the answer, try and think of some information which you can use to approximate the data. For example, a football is a sphere, and a plane might be modelled as a cylinder. You may know these volumes from GCSE Mathematics to be $\pi R^2 H$ for a cylinder and $4/3\ \pi R^3$ for a sphere. You will also need to volunteer estimates for the answers at this point. It is no good simply stating that you know these formulae; what the examiner is looking for is for you to solve the problem by entering approximate values for the objects.

Example answer:

A football is around 20 cm in diameter, and the volume of a sphere is $4/3 \pi R^3$, giving a volume of 0.033 metres cubed. The volume of a cylinder is πR^2 times height, and a plane would be approximately 50 metres long and three metres high, giving 353.3 metres cubed. Therefore, 353.3 divided by 0.033 gives us a total of approximately 10,500 footballs that we could fit into the aeroplane.

Points to note

This demonstrates your core knowledge of science, which is an important but not sufficient attribute for successful applicants. It then goes on to test your application of this knowledge in a situation which you would not ordinarily be familiar with.

How many mobile phone shops are there in the UK? (Geography, Economics)

This question forces you to take a similar approach and begin by taking key principles to build your answer from the ground up.

One technique would be to use areas as samples which are representative and you can then multiply up to give your answer. For example, you could say that on your local high street there are six mobile phone shops, there are two major shopping streets in your borough, and their approximate catchment area is Chiswick in West London, which is one of 32 boroughs in the city. If, for ease of calculation, we treat all boroughs as having equal populations, then an approximate number of people per borough high street would be 6 million divided by 32, which is around 200,000. So if we work with the ratio of 12 mobile phone shops per 200,000 people, and divide this into the population of the UK, which is 60 million, it gives 300 'units' of 200,000 people, so 300 × 12 = 3,600 mobile phone shops.

> Add in qualifiers which show how you are critical of your own assessment. For example, if you say 'Therefore, this is my estimate at present; however, the increase in internet-based sales of mobile phones and second-hand sales from user-based websites such as eBay may mean that this number will gradually decrease over time as the overheads of running a shop cannot compete with the low cost of a primarily online store.'

Data from 2010 shows the number at 4,129 shops, so this is a fairly close estimate; but remember that what you are trying to show is how your mind can explore problems and actively participate in an activity in which you may not have any specialist knowledge whatsoever.

How many animals did Noah take on the Ark? (Biology)

This question requires you to estimate the number of different species of animal and multiply the result by two (one male and one female of each). As always in guesstimate-type questions, you must volunteer an estimate in order for the question to work. Do not worry if it is not exactly correct, as unless it is grossly mistaken, it will allow you to demonstrate your working. The worst type of answer would be 'I don't know' without any reasoning. If you do happen to guess incorrectly, your answer may well be guided by the interview panel, so be prepared to integrate other information that you know, as well as to learn from them.

Points to consider:

- The animal kingdom can be divided into two groups, invertebrates (those without backbones) and vertebrates (those with backbones).

- The majority of the species are insects.

- You may wish to mention the categories you are excluding, such as fish, birds, etc, as they may not have required inclusion on board the Ark, on the basis that they can swim or fly.

- Current scientific estimates would be between 3 and 30 million species. This would mean between 6 and 60 million pairs of animals.

CASE STUDY

A caveat which one student suggested is that if Noah had had more advanced warning in time to build a bigger ark, he would have been best off taking a ratio of two females to one male. This would allow the repopulation of the earth to be undertaken faster (double the rate) for only an increase of 50 per cent loading capacity. This would be more important in animals at the bottom of the food pyramid, so you might choose to bring two female and one male cow, but only one female and one male tiger, so that the rate of production of offspring would more closely mirror the ecological demand in terms of herbivore-to-carnivore ratio. Therefore the student took his estimate of the number of animals and said that Noah would have taken two times this number, but really should have taken around 2.5 times given these conditions. This kind of addition statement can add value and demonstrate good knowledge and application of the knowledge of biology, as well as bringing in concepts from other disciplines, and was very well received. Try to see if you can incorporate the importance of mathematical relationships if relevant.

Is hell exothermic or endothermic? (Chemistry)

Although this looks like a ferociously difficult question, make use of the information and wording of the question to try and guess which academic discipline to draw upon. An earlier question used 'cow' and 'water' to allude to Biology, and 'exothermic' and 'endothermic' should point you towards Chemistry. State your knowledge first, and then go on to develop your argument.

Example answer:

> Hell is commonly depicted as being 'fire and brimstone', which would indicate
> that there are active chemical reactions of combustion being undertaken.
> These reactions are exothermic, with the energy released from the breaking
> of the bonds of the combusting substrate being dispersed into the general
> environment by conduction and convection. However, we cannot assume
> that Hell is exothermic simply because these reactions are going on, as they
> may be needed to maintain the heat in an overall endothermic environment.
> For example, the rate of heat loss may exceed the rate of production of heat
> from this combustion. As to where the heat might go, if Hell is deep underground
> in the centre of the earth, it may be lost into the magma underneath the
> Earth's crust, and used up by, for example, geothermal-energy power stations.
> It may also go to other locations such as Purgatory. Therefore, although the
> presence of combustion reactions suggests an exothermic environment, we
> cannot be sure that hell is not endothermic without considering the possible
> routes of heat loss.

Alternative example answer:

> According to Boyle's Law, if the rate of moles entering Hell is greater than the
> rate of expansion of Hell, then it will be exothermic. Therefore if we model Hell
> as a finite space, and the souls entering it as moles, if the rate of souls entering
> Hell is greater than the rate of its expansion, it will be exothermic. This means
> that Hell will also be exothermic if it is of a fixed size as there should be a steady
> stream of souls entering it. However, if Hell is an expanding space, and its rate
> of expansion is greater than the influx of souls, it would be endothermic.

How high can I climb up a mountain, having eaten only a Mars bar? (Biology, Physics)

The previous two questions have alluded to Biology- and Chemistry-type explanations in turn, and this question is an example of Physics. Physics allows us to relate energy, work done and power and is often useful in simple calculations or estimation of worldly events.

In this case, you would need to first estimate the amount of energy contained within a Mars bar. You may wish to point out that although most energy values that people are concerned about is given in kilocalories, the best unit for relating energy to work done is the kilojoule, and there might be approximately 1,000 kilojoules in a Mars bar. You would then estimate the mass of the person, and state that the gain in gravitational potential energy is equivalent to mass × gravity × height, which would give the equation:

Energy = MGH
1,000,000 Joules (1,000 kilojoules) = 50 × 10 × H
1,000,000 / 500 = H
H = 2,000 metres

For thoroughness, this would be the maximum height you can climb having eaten only a Mars bar. You would then need to subtract estimated losses for many processes such as inefficient absoption in the gut, inefficient transfer to body cells, energy cost for maintaining essential body functions such as cerebral function and respiration, and inefficient use in muscles. You would give rough estimates of these as percentages; for example: 'Of my 1,000 kilojoules of energy, if I estimate that 70 per cent is absorbed in the intestine, which is quite efficient due to its high surface area based on villi, and the fact that only 60 per cent of this energy is available to muscles, and that 50 per cent is lost as heat production as the muscles perform the work, this would leave me 1,000 kilojoules × 0.7 × 0.6 × 0.5 = 210,000 joules.'

Experimental or theoretical design

Experimental or theoretical design questions require a different type of thinking. They offer up a challenge for creating an academically sound 'proof' for a specific set of conditions, such as 'How can you weigh your own head?' Although typically more common in scientific disciplines, you will often find thought experiments or game theory in Economics, Psychology and Politics, such as 'How could you show that time is the key factor which affects people's decisions to help others?' Finally, History, Classics, Archaeology and Anthropology students may be asked how they could prove a theory or fact from the past.

Some of the key principles of answering these types of question are highlighted in examples and explained in the analysis below.

How can you weigh your own head? (Biology, Physics, Engineering, Mathematics)

Example answer:

> If you were in 18th-century France, you could take a weighing scale and a tape measure down to the guillotines every day for a few months and collect data on the weight of heads compared to their circumference, length or any other dimensions. You would plot these data on a graph and you would be able to extrapolate an estimate of your own head based on sample data. For more accurate results, you could stratify the data by sex, age, race and alcohol use (as chronic alcohol abuse can cause cerebral atrophy), and then use a data set which more closely matches that of your profile.

Points to note

It is unlikely that one would be able to undertake this method, but this approach follows a data collection/experimental design method and shows considerable innovation. It also shows an application of your knowledge of statistics to the real world.

Alternative example answer:

> You could set up a fulcrum with a plank of wood and a pivot, and lie on it in a position such that your head was on one side of the pivot, and the body on the other. You could then add weights to the 'head' side of the plank, until it balanced. At this point the moments on both sides of the plank would be equal, one side being 'rest of the body', the other side being 'head + weights'. You could then weigh yourself and calculate the difference in mass between the added weights and the whole body mass, giving the mass for the head.

Points to note

This answer shows good knowledge of mechanics and mathematical ingenuity, as well as the ability to apply information that you know to a problem. Although it might not be 100 per cent accurate (the weight of the head may still be partially supported by the neck, and some of the body mass will be directly over the fulcrum and therefore not exert a moment as its distance is zero), showing your ability to think outside the box is the important point here. If you can mention these limitations in your method, this is even better.

Alternative example answer:

> You could take a 'bottom-up' approach by calculating the various proportions of substances within your head, and then calculate the mass of each. We could

use studies from heads in post mortems to determine the constituents of the head, eg bone, skin, hair, grey and white matter, arteries, veins, blood and connective tissue. We could then use an MRI scan to show the proportions of these materials in the head, and calculate the sum of the masses of each material. The more types of material we take into account, the more accurate our measurement will become.

Point to note

This shows a good knowledge of anatomy and utilization of biological medical knowledge in the answer to the problem.

How could you design an experiment to find out which part of the brain controls emotions? (Psychology, Neurosciences, Philosophy, Anthropology)

You could start by showing a group of people emotive pictures such as happy families and babies, or horrific injuries and war, and find out which areas of the brain are active during their response. One way of doing it would be to use PET scanning (positron emission tomography), which uses radio-labelled glucose injected into the body. This glucose is taken up into areas of activity around the body, and then emits positrons, which collide with electrons to emit gamma rays which can be detected outside the body. Since the brain primarily uses glucose as its energy substrate, you would tell which areas were being used, which might indicate which areas are responsible for emotion.

Other techniques could be to measure the changes in blood flow to certain areas, or use infra-red detectors to highlight areas of heat.

The importance of control groups

In this experiment, what might be the confounding factors? Well, since you are showing the subjects pictures in order to stimulate emotion, it might be that the area of the brain that seems active is the area responsible for, for example, vision or memory. You could try to account for this by having a control group of subjects who are also shown pictures, but rather than emotional ones, they are shown neutral pictures, such as a football, a flower or a table. If the same areas are highlighted, then the areas affected might be accessing memory rather than emotion. You might be able to remove the effect of this by performing the experiment on subjects who were unable to access memory, eg amnesic patients.

You could also try different modalities for stimulating emotion such as auditory triggers – the voice of someone crying, etc. This might enable you to remove any confounding factors related to sensory modality.

OXBRIDGE INTERVIEW KEY POINT

In experimental design questions, it is important that you have a test group, and that you think of a control group with which to compare, to ensure you are getting the results which you think you are. It is important to state the limitations of your study, and any weaknesses or confounding factors. Part of being a good experimental scientist is seeing where experiments might be flawed, and then coming up with solutions for them. If you enjoy this kind of activity and thought process, Oxbridge is the ideal place for you to develop these skills and apply them in cutting-edge research.

Description/explanation-type questions

The second type of question is the description/explanation type, which might be along the lines of 'Tell me about drowning.' These operate in a similar way to the guesstimate questions, but in order to solve them you will use concepts from your scientific knowledge. They will require you to explain your understanding of, for example, the lung, and then extrapolate this knowledge to propose what might be happening when water enters the airways.

When answering such questions, one of the main pitfalls for students is getting the length of answer incorrect. If you decide to ramble on for ages, you run the risk of boring your interview panel by regurgitating relatively basic information they will have heard many times that day, and this disinterest in you will be a major negative selection criterion. If you are too brief, you run the risk of not making clear links between your knowledge and the proposed explanation to the phenomenon. One of the key elements of preparation will therefore be to practise scientific explanation. Activities such as helping others with revision and practising how to explain concepts concisely but accurately will aid in your quest to strike a balance in terms of length.

The best way for you to improve your chances of getting into Oxbridge is not simply to learn how to answer these questions. You should come to love these types of questions, and enjoy the process of stretching your mind to further limits. Oxbridge admissions tutors are looking for intellectually hungry students who are not satisfied simply by learning a syllabus.

If you were a grapefruit, would you prefer to be seedless or non-seedless? (Philosophy, Anthropology, Economics, Biology)

This seems like a rather esoteric question, but allows you as a student to demonstrate the depth of your perception.

The issue here is around natural selection and evolution. For the knowledge element of your answer, it is important to acknowledge the subjects. It can be helpful to think from the perspective of the object in such 'personified' questions, so that you could see what issues might affect you. Try to give a balanced answer including the pros and cons of each, as well as the limitations of your extrapolations, eg to what extent they are true.

Example answer:

As a seedless grapefruit, I would have more appeal as a product to consumers as there is less hassle in eating me. If I was a hedonist, I might choose to be a seedless grapefruit as I might get to experience more luxurious locations, such as a posh restaurant or being made into a juice at a fancy hotel buffet. I would also be the product of genetic engineering, so I could show off to my other grapefruit peers, and I would be the 'fruit' of scientific advancement. However, I would be limited in the experiences of this lifetime as I would not be able to reproduce. Since I as a grapefruit am unable to communicate, I would also be unable to pass on my thoughts, memories and memes to future generations, and I might find this existence quite empty.

If I was a pragmatist, I might wish to be non-seedless, because I would have the chance to replicate and pass on my genetic code. However, I might be condemned to a life in the shelves of a low-budget supermarket, as my appeal as a seeded fruit might be less. Also, I would probably have to die in order for my seeds to be released, so I would never see my 'children' grow up.

I suppose in some ways this dilemma can be compared to couples who are choosing whether or not to have children, or looking at long-term versus short-term gains. At this point, I quite like the idea of the lifestyle of the seedless grapefruit, although this might change.

Tell me about drowning. (Biology, Medicine)

Example answer:

Drowning occurs when your head is under water and you are therefore unable to breathe. The main problem is that breathing is required for the intake of oxygen for aerobic respiration and output of carbon dioxide, which is a waste product of that process. Therefore, when you are not able to make this exchange, there is insufficient oxygen supply for the body. The brain is one of the most sensitive organs to this change, and you may quickly become unconscious and, even if rescued, suffer from brain damage. Water enters the lung as the pressure inside the lungs is lower than the pressure of the water outside. This can be prevented by closing the mouth and sealing the nose, but this can only be maintained whilst you are conscious.

Once unconscious, you would be both unable to save yourself physically by swimming and also unable to prevent water from entering your lungs. This would mean that you could not gain oxygen by diffusion from the air, and as more of your organs failed to receive enough, they would shut down, causing your heart to stop and you to die.

> Approach the question in a systematic way, and use the chance to demonstrate your in-depth knowledge. Refer to specific processes such as aerobic respiration or ion exchange, in order to show that you can communicate comfortably with scientific terminology.

Are humans still evolving? (Philosophy, Politics, Economics, Anthropology, History, Biology)

Consider the following points for use in answering this question:

- Evolution is driven by selection pressures, which are factors which favour the survival of humans with certain traits over others. This causes the surviving humans to pass on their genes more than the non-survivors, giving rise to a change in the average genetic make-up of the population.

- You may argue that many of the traditional selection pressures have been removed from the modern world. Medical technology has allowed humans with conditions which would normally prevent them from surviving to live and reproduce, and therefore the 'survival of the fittest' may no longer be playing an active role in our evolution.

- However, you may argue that there is still selection going on, in terms of selection of partners for reproduction. In First World societies, traits such as physical speed or strength are being surpassed by traits such as intellect in terms of desirability. This may be due to the fact that on average, a higher intellect is often linked to higher earnings compared to, for example, higher strength. Therefore, the average mate selected might be in part due to their earning power, giving a selection advantage to those of higher intellect.

- Further to this, people in higher socio-economic groups have a better life expectancy and therefore are more likely to pass on their genes.

- In the future, you could speculate on traits which may be advantageous for selection. For example, being environmentally conscious may be favourable as fossil fuels become less readily available, and so there may be a 'green' selection pressure in the future.

Point to note

Demonstrate to the admissions tutors that you understand what is meant by evolution, and try to phrase your examples with technical terminology such as 'selection pressures'. This will help the interview panel to see that your answer is directly addressing the question, even if you are being creative with your examples.

Railroad problem

Imagine you are standing by the switch of a train track that splits in two further down the track. On one rail there is a child playing on the track. On the other side there are five children. You are too far away to call out or warn the children in any way, and the train is going to kill the five children on the rail unless you pull the switch. If you do, it will only kill the one child playing by himself. What would you do?

Consider the main contrast:

- Legally, the law does not impose a duty to save the life of another person. Manslaughter through negligence is only imposed when there is duty of care to the person involved, and as a passer-by with no obligation to the individual, there is no chance of prosecution in this case. It is therefore not a crime to let someone die.

- However, this situation becomes more complex with regards to murder if you were to choose to pull the lever to save the five children. Given the situation, there would be a degree of premeditation to the act you would undertake, and certainly there is a direct causality between your action and their deaths. This action would leave you open to a charge of murder.

- Ethically, under utilitarianist principles, in order to maximize the greatest good for the greatest number, you should press the switch to minimize the harm of this train accident.

- Because of this complex ethical problem, you may find that the crown prosecutor, judge and jury are sympathetic to your case in terms of charging and sentencing. However, the legal grounds for prosecution remain.

- Therefore one way to view the 'optimal' solution is pull the lever, save the lives of five at the price of one, but not get caught. However, if the situation was changed to involve stabbing a wealthy person to steal money to save 100 people, you may find that this seems far more abhorrent; however, the principles are the same. Therefore, using deontological ethics (focusing on the actions rather than the results, in contrast to utilitarianism), you may find that you do not wish to pull the lever after all.

What medical conditions might vampires be suffering from that might explain their particular characteristics? (Biology, Medicine)

This question seems very difficult at first, but references to popular culture and science are becoming increasingly common and this type of question is not unheard of. The process of answering such questions should be first to consider what makes a vampire special and then compare them to what you know from biology and chemistry.

Example answer:

The main characteristics of vampires are that they drink human blood, are pale, cannot stand sunlight, garlic or holy water. The first two characteristics may be linked, as human beings who are pale sometimes have anaemia, which is a low concentration of haemoglobin in the blood. I have seen doctors checking under the eyelids of patients to see if it is particularly white, as this is a sign of anaemia. Therefore, vampires might require a source of haemoglobin, which may come from human blood. In a hospital this is acquired by blood transfusion, which goes directly into the veins, as it might be damaged by the acid and enzymes in the stomach. However, if vampires had an adaptation to avoid this damage, such as that they could absorb the haemoglobin via their digestive tract, alleviating their anaemia, I can therefore speculate that their blood is being used up in some way, as they need to feed quite often.

With regards to avoiding sunlight, they could have a photosensitivity, which is one of the signs of meningitis, which is an infection of the layers surrounding the brain. They might alternatively have another disease, such as xeroderma pigmentosum, which vastly increases the chance of a person getting skin cancer on exposure to UV light which is present in sunlight.

The avoidance of garlic may be due to a simple allergy to a biological component of garlic, such as certain acids contained within it. Finally, the aversion to holy water is the most difficult to explain, but it may be a confounding factor, as the water may be blessed in a metal or stone container of some kind, and therefore contain dissolved minerals which cause a reaction in a vampire.

> You may not be entirely correct, but if you can justify your answer as well as accept criticism and learn new facts from your interviewers, you will be able to engage in an interesting interaction that will increase your chances of selection.

Who is your favourite scientist, and why? (Physical Sciences)

Example answer:

My favourite scientist is Archimedes, the ancient Greek mathematician. The Archimedes screw, the tool for raising water which he is most famous for, I actually find the least interesting achievement, as it can be considered a simple practical device of agriculture, which is important, but not irreplaceable by other water-raising systems, most likely to be the use of slaves back in his day. The reason he is my favourite scientist is in part due to the fact that I am a keen water-skier, and as a youth, my parents would take me to various beaches around the world to let me follow my passion. I always took it for granted that I would stay afloat, but when I began to think about how it was possible, I could not explain it myself. Although I learned in school about the Archimedes principle that an object immersed in a fluid experiences a buoyant force that is equal in magnitude to the force of gravity on the displaced fluid, I could not imagine that someone could discover this for the first time purely by his own calculations. I admire the way that his mind pursued the mathematical and scientific modelling of observations in real life. His further achievements, including the calculation of the volume of a sphere, are still useful to this very day, and I hope to adopt his curiosity and scientific approach to real-life phenomena in my future studies.

Try not only to describe the achievements and discoveries of your nominated scientist, but also link these in with your interests.

Other scientists you may like to research include:

Charles Darwin;

Albert Einstein;

Isaac Newton;

Nicola Tesla;

Thomas Edison;

Francis Crick and James Watson;

Leonardo da Vinci;

Edward Jenner.

If you were in charge of the country, would you encourage or discourage the population as a whole to have sex, and why? (Politics, Economics, Geography, Anthropology)

This question is quite an unusual proposition, but remember to give a full account of the pros and cons of both sides before coming to your balanced conclusion.

Consider the following issues:

Pro-sex position:

- More sex leads to more babies, which would eventually increase the proportion of working to non-working population and give a better economic profile to the population.
- In the event of war, there would be a larger young population for conscription.
- More freely available sex may reduce the need for sex-trade workers, eg prostitutes, with the associated crime and victimization of women.

Anti-sex position:

- There may be an increase in sexually transmitted diseases.
- Morally, certain religious beliefs might consider this wrong, particularly if it occurred outside marriage.
- The population of the country is in decline, and there may not be a need for a 'baby boom'. If considered in the extreme, the country might not have enough resources or the infrastructure to support a hugely growing population.

Example questions and answers for Arts and Humanities

As you will have seen from above, scientists are fortunate in some ways that there are some key principles, landmark experiments and prominent figures which can be referred to as examples to answer certain interview questions. The breadth of this knowledge is certainly quite significant, but for Arts and Humanities students it is broader still. You will therefore need to take a different approach from that of your scientific colleagues.

On the positive side, this means that there is less by way of 'necessary' reading; it is far more general than this. In fact, in subjects such as History or English Literature there is little reading which would not be of some use. Nevertheless, the same theory applies in what to do with your reading material. Make sure that you have a good understanding of the reading you have done, and make a brief 'interview-ready' summary of the key facts and arguments in your reading. For literary subjects, you may wish to note down the key influences and parallels which you can refer to during the interview.

When revising for the Arts and Humanities it is vital that you appreciate the contrast in opinions to those of your own. This is because you may very well be presented with them, or challenged by the interviewers once you express them, and you must expect to have to justify each assertion that you make.

For most students, you will have a very limited memory for direct quotations. Use this space very carefully indeed, and if you do wish to remember useful quotes, try to limit them to around 10 at most. After all, the interview is concerned with creating a dialogue between two academics, and preparation involving direct memorization is likely to be less useful, and not in keeping with the theme of the assessment. A well-chosen and timely quote can add a sparkle to an already good interview answer, but does not suffice for the main body of your answer.

Subject-specific advice

Classics

Example questions:

'What is it that makes you want to study dead languages rather than useful ones?'

'What contemporary literature do you read?'

'Who is your favourite classical author, and why?'

'Who is the more important to us today; Livy or Cicero?'

Worked example: 'Tell me about the roles of Classical civilizations and modern culture, particularly entertainment and media.'

The depiction of Classical civilization, from the obvious examples such as the decadent savagery depicted by Robert Graves in *I, Claudius* to the films, television series and documentaries which capture people's attention is based on our study and understanding of that world. I think to many people this period of time is so interesting because it was an advanced world of philosophy and science for an ancient time; however, it also possessed a certain tabloidesque penchant for drama. Even the profligation of medical dramas on television has a connection to the Classical world; after all, the etymology of their terminology often lies in classical roots. All of these examples underpin the importance to me of the study of the culture and languages of this fascinating period; in fact, I can go so far as to say my interest in Latin and Ancient Greek may well have started from my exposure to Classical content in modern culture, and I am certainly interested to study this 'the other way around' and learn more about how Classics do indeed affect our day-to-day life.

English

Example questions:

'Tell me about your favourite book.'

'Who is your favourite author? Give some examples of authors who have a *contrasting* style, and why you prefer your chosen author.'

'Read this passage; tell me what you think.'

'Why should we be interested in popular modern literature such as the "Twilight" series?'

Worked example: 'Who is your favourite author?'

Edgar Allan Poe is my favourite author because of his consistency between his literary beliefs and his own writing style; it is particularly interesting to read works such as 'The Raven' and then to read the accompanying essay 'The Philosophy of Composition', which lays out his methodology and shows how he went about constructing this very distinctive piece of work. It is amazing to realize what a benefit to future students of his writing this would go on to be, and reading this pair of works helped me to understand at a very early stage that being a creator of literature should allow you to be a student of it too, and vice versa. I am perhaps looking to take the same approach to Poe, who was famous in his time for his criticism skills as opposed to his writing.

You can see how this particular student used their additional reading journal to prepare for their interview; she has managed to summarize the key points briefly and succinctly, and rather than simply focusing on one piece of work, she links two of the author's contributions, which are very different in nature. The student is also following the Specificity rule for Oxbridge interview questions by giving precise examples of the author's works rather than simply naming an author or style. She has managed to see the unseen question, which is 'Who is your favourite author *and why*?' A brief answer, just naming the author, or even the author and a piece of work, is simply not enough. You can imagine that the admissions tutor would have to follow up those questions with further questions; here the student gives a complete answer which is not too long-winded, and opens the floor for *discussion*, which is where she can get even further ahead of her competitors by working in a *supervision or tutorial-like environment* with the tutor.

In the later discussion, you may wish to use other references which you have read, for example the criticism of this work by T S Eliot, who felt that there were some disparities between Poe's writing and his description. How far do you feel this criticism is valid? Do you think that the 'recipe' for writing poetry or prose should come before it is laid down on paper? It is not how we currently study literature, as we would expect our study to be the opposite way round, by analysing a piece of text and then seeing what devices and messages lie within.

History

Example questions:

> 'Give examples of when lessons *have not* been learned from history, and mistakes have been repeated.'

> 'Have revolutions changed? How so?'

> 'As far as you are concerned, what is the most significant event in history?'

> 'How will you describe the impact of the 9/11 attacks to your children?'

Worked example: 'What makes a good historian? Do you have what it takes to meet the standards you have described?'

> To me, history is the art of pursuing the truth and recording it as objectively as possible. A good historian would be able to perceive and record this information, taking into account as far as possible the undue influences that were affecting him at that time. Therefore, I am critical enough to say that I would not be objective enough to comment on my own objectivity; being myself, I would be easily influenced by bias. However, there may be some measures which are useful to us in this regard; for example my performance in History examinations and winning the sixth-form Arthur Ledwie prize for History – these may offer some independent measure of my ability to be objective. However, my answer is no, I do not yet meet the standard which I have described because it would be paradoxical – a historian should never be satisfied with the current level of their ability. I would say that I have an awareness of objectivity, a high standard of written communication and critical appraisal of all information which I intend to use, but also that I hope to develop these skills for many years to come in this college.

This student begins by expressing his overall understanding of history as an academic discipline before going on to apply it to himself. He uses a clever rhetorical device about being 'objective enough to comment on' his 'own objectivity', whereby he manages to demonstrate his communication skills to the interviewer whilst at the same time underlining an important point in the theory of history: self assessment.

History of Art

Example questions:

'What is art?'

'Who is your favourite artist?'

'Tell me about artists whom you dislike. Why?'

'Compare and contrast these images.'

Worked example: 'How could you argue that increased university fees reflect society's decrease in the perceived value of art?'

For all the value that art has in establishing cultural connections, bridging gaps and communication across generations, it is sometimes perceived as having less practical value to society than, for example, the study of sciences. This should not always be the case; the invention of the television is a scientific marvel which I do not understand the workings of, but nevertheless it would be of far less value to society if it were not for the film, drama and even advertising that is conducted through this medium. The increase in university fees affects all subjects equally; however, the earning potential of a student in Economics who goes on to work in a bank is far greater than a student who hopes to study Art History and write as a critic in the future. Therefore, the cost to myself is far greater than to those students; in the past the study of art in all forms would be more supported by the government, and now this is perhaps less so. Nevertheless, as I believe we pursue study in our passions and not for monetary gains, I do not believe this will affect the arts community as much as it has been portrayed; if anything, it helps those of us who are applying to ensure that we really do love the subject, and I for one am actually rather grateful for that.

Linguistics and Modern and Medieval Languages

Example questions:

'How does knowledge of the author affect our interpretation of their works?'

'Is humour different in different languages?'

'Is learning languages a talent?'

'What is grammar?'

Worked example: 'How would you attempt to communicate with an alien who has just landed on the planet?'

I think it would be a difficult situation, but one which I would initially address as I would talking to a foreign person from a country which I am not too familiar with. This is on the basis that the alien does not know my language, but has a language of his own and can infer some information from the basic principles of a language. I would therefore focus on elements of language which are universal or commonplace to man; in this particular setting, tone, simple grammar and clear indication of proper nouns. The first thing which comes to mind is a greeting which would simply be 'Hello' and an introduction whereby I point to myself and say my name, and point to the alien as if to ask what theirs is. However, despite my fascination with language as the spoken and written medium, I should be aware that body language could play an important role, as the alien may not even have ears. I would therefore try to express myself in a friendly manner through both gestures and voice, so as to not put myself in danger.

Music

Example questions:

'Describe the work of composers whom you dislike. Why is this the case?'

'What role has music played within human society?'

'How can the instrument that we play affect the interpretation of a piece of music?'

Worked example: 'Can you describe the relationship between music and mathematics?'

To me, music is a method of communication, but in order to understand its basis, we can think about the fundamentals of music; time, rhythm, meter and harmony. All of these can also be understood in terms of mathematics, perhaps the most complex being the numerical relationship between frequencies which we see in scales, and it is on this basis that we can tune musical instruments to the correct pitch. Mathematics is a science, which helps us to understand the world we live in. I see music as having the very same role, facilitating the understanding of our world and ourselves, but as an art.

Summary

- The study of all interview questions holds common principles which admissions tutors look for; therefore it is vital to look outside your own subject.

- Guesstimate questions require you to *volunteer* approximations and show your working.

- Experimental design questions can be addressed with academically cautious proposals.

- Description/explanation questions should allow you to demonstrate the depth and breadth of your knowledge.

- Arts and Humanities students should prepare for reviewing unseen literature.

- Contrasting opinions should always be studied and volunteered.

- Keep some direct quotations up your sleeve, but do not focus too heavily on this aspect.

CHAPTER 13

Speech, language and vocabulary

- Speaking the same language as your admissions tutors
- Vocabulary development activities
- The unimportance of accent
- The importance of grammar

Excellent verbal communication skills will help you to impress admissions tutors and impart your arguments effectively. Therefore, it is important to work on these skills through a variety of exercises. Language and vocabulary development is an area which most students will not specifically work on but can greatly enhance your own interview performance; use this chapter to gain yet another competitive edge over your fellow applicants.

Speaking the same language as your admissions tutors

Academics in each specialist field have methods of communicating their work to one another: at presentations, conferences, in e-mails, literature and so on. It is important for their work that their use of terminology is consistent, in order to make all of their communications efficient as well as consistent. Therefore, each subject will contain its own set of vocabulary which is used by academics for this very purpose.

This set of vocabulary is a potentially important resource for applicants to tap into. It can give you the edge over other students who have not considered this additional method of preparing for interview. First, much like communications that admissions tutors do on a daily basis, it saves many words and makes your conversation more streamlined. Second, it shows an interest in the subject that you have taken time to learn its specialized language. Last, it gives a more professional impression, and as a result you would be comfortable speaking to your fellow students, and potentially as a future researcher or teacher in the field.

What is the best way to go about acquiring this new set of words? As usual, there is somewhat of a divide between the Sciences and the Arts and Humanities.

Sciences

As with most processes, in preparing for a Science subject application, the starting procedure is knowing your AS- and A-level material inside out. You will come across many of the knowledge elements here if you read in proper depth; make sure you analyse each definition to ensure that you fully understand what it means *and how it is commonly used*.

However, in addition to this, you will also come across terms which you may not be so familiar with as part of your additional Oxbridge reading, whether in books, online, in journals or by listening to a documentary or lecture. Whenever you read or hear 'linear', 'laminar', 'turbulent', 'asymptotic', 'symbiotic', 'embolus', 'Pareto efficient', 'optimal' or any of the hundreds of scientific terms used to describe phenomena, write them down. Start to create your own glossary of words which you can then later look up. Once again, it is important to put a context to each term. How did you see or hear it used by the author or speaker? Knowing when to use the term, and when not to, are both equally important.

Arts and humanities

For Arts subjects, the principles are very similar to start with, ie using your school-level material and being very comfortable with the common terminology used in your subject, such as literary techniques. Perhaps more than for science students, it can be useful to have a few examples to mind when you are creating your glossary. You may have favourite examples of 'hyperbole', 'litotes', 'pathos', 'assonance', various meters of verse and so on. These will give you a great perspective on any material that may come up in interview, and more importantly your use of them will reassure the interviewer that you have not simply memorized definitions but have taken a more cultured approach to the learning of your discipline.

Staying in the classroom environment, you may find your teacher a particularly good source for broadening vocabulary; discuss interesting pieces of work or concepts with them, and see how they choose to describe their views. In addition to this, you will need to look further afield. You may wish to refer to book reviews, opinion articles and other critical work from leading academics. In particular, look for how these intellectuals critically appraise a piece of work. How do they express their opinions with regards to the material, and what are the terms which they use for doing so? As you read more, you will appreciate the *quantitative* element of this skill; to what degree they express agreement or dissatisfaction, whether vehement or mild. You will find styles that you especially like and dislike, and you can start to form your own unique take on these basic principles.

As a rule, cross-disciplinary learning of vocabulary can be very helpful indeed in both written and interview settings. Why? It is because it is the most efficient way to demonstrate the *breadth* of your knowledge. As we have seen in Chapter 9, both depth and breadth of knowledge are critical, and whilst comfortable use of specialized vocabulary in your own discipline is a sign of *depth*, touching on concepts from neighbouring or even distant subjects really allows you to show off the range or breadth.

Therefore, use the subject-axis table of allied subjects in Chapter 12. In particular, Physics and Mathematics have such a significant degree of overlap that you must be fluently versed in both.

Economics and Politics are an example of a pair of subjects that are intimately linked; crudely understood, the decisions of governments are often based on economics, and they often have consequences on the economy. However, students in both disciplines should also be comfortable discussing the effect of one on the other, and Economics students should be very comfortable in Mathematics and Statistics terminology. This principle is even more critical when studying compound subjects such as Politics, Psychology and Sociology (Cambridge) or Politics, Philosophy and Economics (Oxford).

As a last point of caution, I cannot overemphasize the importance of maintaining a good level of understanding of the terms you are about to use. Reference to historical work can sometimes be useful, but be careful with how you use it. For example, if you refer to 'Schrodinger's cat', it is important that you understand the background in which this thought experiment was created and what it implies. You will not get away with superficial knowledge; but at the same time, if you can succinctly explain the terms and vocabulary that you choose, this will demonstrate your interest and ability in the subject and give you an invaluable edge over the less-prepared candidate.

Vocabulary development activities

Listening to well-spoken academics is a good way to become comfortable with the technical language before your interview. One of the best ways to find talks that are interesting and which may help your language skills are those given at the Technology, Entertainment and Design conferences (TED). These talks are given by renowned academics on fascinating topics, and all are available online at www.ted.com, a huge free lecture database. It is a fantastic resource, and also allows you to branch out into similar fields and broaden your range of knowledge.

> Listening to your favourite talks *more than* once is something which can help to reinforce the ideas in them, but you will also become familiar with the content, allowing you to focus more on the techniques used to present the ideas.

Read up-to-date research or literature in your subject. (Please refer to Chapter 12 for subject-specific advice on additional reading.) This will introduce you to terms that are used commonly as well as give a context for how they are used. Always look up such terms in a dictionary or specific resource for your subject to make sure you understand their exact meanings.

Interview language checklist

- DO create a vocabulary list for interview, including both definitions and example uses in context.

- DO practise using some of the terms with your teachers and peers, in your answers and discussion.

- DO use an appropriate amount of specialist vocabulary in your answers; avoid using too much, and make sure you mix in plenty of 'lay person' explanations to demonstrate to the admissions tutors that you have a good fundamental understanding of their questions.

- DO listen to top academics discussing their subjects.

- DO NOT artificially force the use of technical vocabulary into your answers. This may make it seem as if you are trying to impress the examiners with verbal tricks rather than demonstrating your understanding of the language used by experts in the field.

The unimportance of accent

Many students worry about their accent, be it international or regional, and some even go so far as to ask for coaching or elocution lessons.

I have posed this question to several admissions tutors, and they have reassured me that accent will play no role in student selection. In fact, for many international students who are managing to communicate sophisticated arguments in a language which is not their mother tongue, it is even more impressive.

The importance of grammar

As long as your accent is comprehensible, it will pose you no problems. You should be more concerned with the actual content of your speech. Ask yourself the following questions. Do you make grammatical or sense errors? Do you find people correcting your answers in terms of tense, person or quantitatively (the degree to which you make your assertations)? These will make it more difficult to communicate a well-reasoned argument to your admissions tutors, and should be the focus of your work in terms of language. In particular, try to gain a contextual sense of how quantitative relationships are conveyed, using words such as 'extremely', 'marginally', 'approximately', 'roughly', 'mostly', 'somewhat' and so on.

Summary

- Every subject has its own terminology with which you must become intimately familiar.

- Create your own glossary of terms from what you read and hear.

- Ensure you understand the meanings of and appropriate contexts for technical terms.

- For interviews, try listening to lectures and talks to hear pronunciation as well as how specialist terms are used.

- Don't waste time correcting your accent unless you are totally incomprehensible.

- Spend time working on accurate sense and grammar.

CHAPTER 14

Fees, funding and bursaries

- General considerations
- Oxbridge-specific bursaries and opportunities
- College-dependent funding

Fees and funding are now two of the key issues in university applications due to recent changes in government policy that allow universities to charge a large amount to students in order to make up for the removal of government support. This chapter explains how this affects you, some special opportunities at Oxbridge for funding, and a guide to how to take advantage of college-based funding to further reduce your costs.

General considerations

Both Oxford and Cambridge have increased their fees to £9,000 per year, which is the maximum cost for universities in the UK. However, there are several important points to bear in mind.

Many other top institutions are now charging this fee

This means that although you will be paying top dollar for your education, you are unlikely to find any top-ranking university offering a significant economic advantage. Therefore, if you are going to pay a large amount for a university education, it may as well be the best that you can possibly get.

The Oxbridge difference: in a market of high-priced universities, Oxbridge's excellent teaching, research and education make it the most desirable choice of the UK's elite universities.

Value for money

Many students complain, and go so far as to protest, about the apparent lack of value for money that this increased fee represents. They calculate that their teaching time, which can be only a few hours of lectures per week, amounts to hundreds of pounds per hour, and that this is unacceptable. It is vital to bear in mind, however, that it is not simply the cost of the lectures that is incurred; maintaining research, overheads of the teaching locations, setting and marking examinations and design of the course material all need to be considered.

The Oxbridge difference: even if you feel that there are relatively few lectures, you will certainly appreciate that regular, two-to-one tutorials with leaders in the field can help justify the cost.

Repayment starts only after you start earning

Oxford and Cambridge are committed to widening access to education, and the fact that there is no up-front payment of fees means that everyone can 'afford' them at the time when they are deciding on a degree. Whether the degree is worth the debt is perhaps a more difficult question, but in the long term, earnings for graduates compared to non-graduates will mean that you are likely to make far more this way, in addition to the value of your education. I encourage all students not to be too short-sighted with this; £27,000 sounds daunting indeed at this stage in your life, but as your career progresses you may find that this amount, taken over many years, holds much less fear for you. A further education, and especially an Oxbridge one, should be considered a prudent investment for your own future.

The Oxbridge difference: investing in your long-term earning potential is best done at Oxbridge, as graduate prospects are universally amongst the best in the UK. Therefore, you will be getting a better chance of employment, with a higher starting salary, compared to your peers who are attending another university at the same price.

Additional bursaries

There are a number of government-approved, means-tested bursaries in all universities. However, Oxbridge has a vast number of additional options for you which will not be available at other institutions. This is partly due to the collegiate system, which provides further support independent from the university, and also due to the huge number of wealthy benefactors who bequeath generous sums to support bright students from disadvantaged backgrounds.

The Oxbridge difference: the sheer range of opportunities and support at Oxbridge is unparalleled in the UK.

Oxbridge-specific bursaries and opportunities

Student loans

The Student Loans Company (SLC) provides loans for you to cope with the living cost at university. It is important to note that these are separate from fees, but you will have to pay back the money after graduation and when you begin working. However, payment is taken as a percentage of your income, so you will never be burdened with a lump sum or sudden invoice.

Maintenance grant

At present this is £2,906 for a student from a household with income less than £25,000; household income between £25,000 and £50,000 will qualify the student for a reduced amount. You will never have to repay any of your maintenance grant. (For further information, go to www.direct.gov.uk and browse the education and learning section for up-to-date figures.)

Bursaries

Oxbridge make bursaries available for students on a means-tested basis, similarly to the maintenance grant. The assessment will be undertaken by your local education authority (LEA) after filling in some forms on family income; once these are complete, it is the only assessment you will need for both the government-based maintenance grant and the university-based bursary.

At present this bursary amounts to £3,400 per year. This is a rather large sum of money which is available to you essentially free of charge, and unique to Oxbridge.

Scholarships

In Oxbridge this term can have several meanings, and each one needs to be addressed slightly differently.

University-wide scholarships

In Cambridge, for example, the National Scholarship Programme is a scheme for students from means-tested disadvantaged backgrounds, which grants a fee waiver of £6,000 in the first year in addition to the various grants and bursaries detailed above.

You will be eligible if your household income is less than £21,000 and, in addition to this, you have spent more than six months in care, have a disability, are a single parent or have an entitlement to free school meals. In this case, you will not need to apply in advance and you will be given the chance to apply for this scholarship once you have received an offer from the university. Oxford has a number of university-wide scholarships, details of which can be found on its website; there are different ones available depending on your place of birth, including those specifically for Europe, Asia and Africa. There may be specific scholarship forms which you must attend to; make sure you read up very thoroughly.

College scholarships

Scholarships in the college setting are slightly different from the university-wide variety, and tend to be smaller amounts based on your performance in examinations. If you gain a First in an end-of-year examination, or come top in the college, there are various awards in the order of a few hundred pounds, in addition to the prestige the awards carry.

CASE STUDY   Oriel College, Oxford

The full range of financial support is best understood by looking at an example college. Oriel College, Oxford, like most colleges, has a *Hardship Grant* fund for students in financial difficulties. The *Oriel College Development Trust Bursaries* are also available, which amount to £500–£1,500 per year, and are for students from families with lower incomes. Financial awards for performance in examinations can amount to £200 per year. The college has a number of grants available for travel, language courses and even vacation grants, as long as a worthwhile pursuit is intended that may be related to your field of study or otherwise academically beneficial.

Each college has a wealth of information on funding available on its website, and it is important that you check for potential bursaries, scholarships and grants that can help you manage your finances at university.

Long holidays

One of the other 'fringe' financial benefits of the Oxbridge system is that you have long breaks, particularly over summer, which can be used to find employment and bolster your coffers for the terms. You may find the reputation of the universities actually helps you in getting a job, and this can be enhanced by expanding your CV with positions of responsibility such as involvement in running a student society or union.

You may find quite lucrative opportunities which are offered at Oxbridge by virtue of careers fairs; major financial institutions, management consultants, banks and accounting firms will all be having recruitment drives. The careers service will also provide help with how to formulate a CV and cover letter. If you do gain a placement over summer, the payment can be similar to that of a first-year graduate (pro rata) and this adds up to substantial earnings, as well as the invaluable experience and potential for future employment. Second-year students in particular often look to internships or employment over summer as a method of increasing their chances of success when applying for jobs at the end of their degree.

Organ scholars and Choral scholars

The chapels of colleges in Oxbridge are renowned worldwide for their architecture and history; however, they also gain this reputation for the musicians who perform within them. This is why Organ and Choral scholars have a particular system of application.

If you are reading this book near to application time, you will either be a strong candidate for such a position due to your musical ability, or not at all. There is no scope for any sort of short-term attempt to gain this type of scholarship; the colleges are looking for the absolute best and most talented musicians, who also have the great intellectual capacity which is expected of all Oxbridge students. Most candidates will already be performing at a high level, at least within their school, but most probably also beyond. Therefore, it is more important for those select individuals to focus on the academic side of the application to ensure that this does not let them down. This is where the principles in this book will prove invaluable: everything from the UCAS personal statement to aptitude tests, written work and the interview must be given due attention *in addition to maintaining musical excellence*.

Uniquely, applying for an Organ or Choral scholarship allows you to apply to both Oxford and Cambridge within one application – this is, of course, not possible for all other applicants. This indicates how scarce such scholars are as well as how high is the regard in which they are held. If you are reading this with more than a year to go, and you already enjoy singing or playing the organ to a high level, you may wish to actively seek out activities which can improve your performance as well as demonstrating your ability to admissions tutors. These can range from concerts for organizations or charities to extra lessons and tours abroad. This is a very serious commitment, however, and you will need to invest a great deal of time to stand any serious chance of gaining a place. Please bear in mind that each college usually has around two organ scholars in residence at any given time and no more than two dozen choral scholars. You will also need to undertake a competitive test in your discipline to gain a place.

College-dependent funding

There are many ways in which your college can save you money whilst you are in residence, and you can factor these into your financial planning if you are having monetary concerns.

Individual funding

Most colleges will have ways to help you meet many of the day-to-day costs of university life, particularly if you excel in academic, creative or sporting arenas. Book grants are quite commonplace, although you may not always need them because of access to college, departmental and university libraries. These are supported by a growing collection of online resources.

Sports funds are often based on merit; if you represent a college or university team, your college will often support you by providing some, or even all, of your costs. This can be a huge boon in joining clubs which have relatively expensive 'subscriptions' to take part in, or sports which require expensive consumable goods such as shuttlecocks or tennis balls.

Projects funding

In addition to these day-to-day funds, there are special funds set aside to help students pursue activities which are deemed worthwhile. These can include trips abroad for volunteering, language courses, charity work or teaching, but can include other more exotic options such as shooting a low-budget film or producing an informational newsletter for the public. The decisions are made by a committee involved in the college's finances and academia, and are made on the basis of letters written. Therefore, once you have a good idea, refine it and then apply for funding; the worst that could happen is that they will say no, and you will also hone your application and writing techniques in the process.

Academic prizes

The majority of these fit the description of a college-based scholarship as described above. However, in addition to this, there are a number of competitions run by many colleges which involve essay writing, problem solving, reviews or composition (either literary or musical). These also have prizes associated with them which can also range into hundreds of pounds, which is a worthwhile endeavour to pursue for many students.

Food

Food is often subsidized within colleges, and is therefore a cheap and fast way to get your nutrition as well as keeping down costs. Most colleges charge a kitchen fixed charge (KFC) of around £90 to £130 per term to cover the costs of running the hall. This can seem like a lot, but you are then able to get breakfast or lunch for £2 to £3, and dinner for only slightly more, at £3 to £4. Furthermore, eating in hall can help you to socialize with collegemates from different disciplines and enjoy a wonderful setting to dine in.

CASE STUDY   Gonville and Caius College, Cambridge

This particular college operates a slightly unusual system, in that it includes as part of the termly bill a fee for a fixed number of dinner tickets. It is an interesting case study because it does in fact force you to dine in hall, which is not seen in most other colleges. This policy benefits the society of the college – students will be brought together at the dinner table on a regular basis. However, it does limit your dining options and you must use your dinner tickets lest they become wasted at the end of the term, which can be somewhat frustrating. Nevertheless, most students are quite happy with this and setting aside £6.05 for 40 dinners despite the relative restriction, is fairly easy; if nothing else, it will give you a common topic to complain about with your fellow collegemates!

College bars

These are another area in which you can make a significant saving compared to going out on the town, although I am loath to offer any further encouragement on this topic as an educator and medical professional. Just be prepared for rock-bottom prices!

Accommodation

Oxford and Cambridge Colleges provide accommodation for all years of your under-graduate study, and also for a significant proportion of graduate study years. One of the best things is the range of options available to you; for those looking to economize, you can choose to steer clear of the large, ensuite, central rooms and prepare for something more cosy.

The next thing is that after your first year, your room can be chosen according to ballot. This can be a random draw, or it can be based on your academic performance. This is yet another advantage for the hard-working student as you will have a free choice of the best, or the cheapest, options in college.

The bottom line

As you can see, college life can be made far easier by a number of different options which you may well not have been aware of. However, it is absolutely vital to do your research in this area as you may have to apply for means testing, student loans, and to the college itself, depending on the circumstances. The good news is that the information needed is almost always on the college website, and each college has a specific page entitled 'Finances' or similar. This will allow you to rapidly compare the resources available for you. Furthermore, if you have questions which have not been answered by the internet, you can contact the college office or the Junior Bursar for more details. The bottom line is that for students from less-well-off backgrounds, you will find yourself very well supported at Oxbridge, perhaps more so than at other universities, and financial issues should not be something that put you off from pursuing a course of study if you are capable.

Summary

- Do your research early, as Oxbridge has multiple sources of financial support for students.

- There are many sources of funding within colleges in addition to government and university aid.

- Subsidized accommodation and food can help make university life more manageable.

- Funding for sports, books and particular projects is often available.

- Study for money: prizes often have a monetary as well as academic value for high achievers.

CHAPTER 15

International students

- Alumni and fellow country networks
- Demonstrating independence
- Additional personal statement advice

International students face a particularly difficult challenge when applying to Oxbridge. First, there are limited numbers of places for a larger number of applicants when compared to home students; this makes the competition even more ferocious. You will be required to communicate in a language which may not be your mother tongue, or indeed one which you may not have been taught your subject in. You may need to pass a language competency test to a high level; this adds yet another barrier which must be overcome. Fees are high compared to those for local students, and you may wish to apply for scholarships and bursaries, which adds a further layer of complexity to the entire process. Nevertheless, there are some specific activities which you can undertake to enhance your chances.

Alumni and fellow country networks

There is no doubt that students from overseas blend in very comfortably to the overall society in the Oxbridge environment. This is particularly enhanced by the social element of the college environment, as well as various societies and activities which promote mixing with other cultures. Indeed, there is a society for almost every ethnic group or nationality which you might belong to, which addresses your specific needs as an individual. Despite being a local student, I myself was a member of many such societies during my time at university, particularly to take part in events that involved the eating of traditional foods. However, their main role was to develop a great sense of community and support within nationals of their country, and this is something which you as an applying student can certainly take advantage of in several ways, as noted below.

Direct contact

You will be able to locate the student society website for your home country, which will give you access to important information as well as contact details for the key figures within that society: the committee members. These represent the student body from your country and therefore may be a useful port of call if you have any specific questions with regards to applying.

There are some rules and customs to bear in mind whilst contacting student societies, which I encourage you to adhere to:

- Try to make contact at a time which is convenient for the people you will contact. People will be far too busy to lend a sympathetic ear during exam term (Easter until June), but during holidays represents a good opportunity.

- Students tend to be home for summer holidays, and many will also return for the Christmas holidays. Many students are unlikely to go back over Easter as exams will be looming. Of these holiday periods, summer is the longest and will not involve imminent exams; therefore you are most likely to be able to meet up with contacts during this time.

- The president of a student society is their elected representative, and therefore may reasonably be expected to deal with queries from potential future members of that society. However, you may also find that the society secretary is a good person to contact as they are responsible for general correspondence.

- There may be events held by the society, or indeed by the university itself in your country. Look very carefully for these well in advance (typically over summer), and make sure your schedule is cleared to attend them.

Double your information by contacting members from both Oxford and Cambridge, and attending events for both. You may find that there are common points made by both; these are clearly very important and must be paid attention to. There may also be additional points which may be overlooked by one group or the other; these may give you the upper hand compared to your peers who simply attend one of the events. It will also allow you to meet more role models and successful candidates, and therefore the sensible student will try to take as much information on board as they can.

Demonstrating independence

Local students may come from all corners of the UK, and therefore can be some distance away from their home. Nevertheless, they are less prone to culture shock than foreign students, and will still maintain some degree of social support from their home environment, including an ability to contact family and friends unimpeded by time difference or excessive cost. International students will have to overcome cultural differences, and in an Oxbridge setting this must occur very quickly as term times are very short and intense.

Therefore, in addition to your intellectual abilities, you must also demonstrate to the admissions tutors that you are capable of adapting quickly to cope with a new environment in order to succeed.

This is best done if you can demonstrate your ability to operate independently and in an environment which is not familiar to you. If you have the chance to plan ahead, some activities which can be helpful include the following:

Foreign exchange programmes. These can be useful in showing your ability, and can also convince yourself that an overseas programme of study is the right course for you. This assuredness in your own decision will come across well both in interview and in the personal statement.

Summer language programmes. Similarly to foreign exchange programmes, these have the additional benefit of specifically improving your language skills; this will be invaluable at the interview but also in showing your commitment and long-term planning for your final university destination.

Charity work overseas. You may wish to undertake some voluntary service in a foreign country, both as part of your own spectrum of interests as well as to further your own personal development. It is important to research this well in advance, and in doing so you can uncover other opportunities to demonstrate your independence and ability to cope with life abroad. This option is one of the most flexible as it caters for almost any interest: you could teach Science, Maths or a language in a developing nation, do more physical work such as constructing a school or hospital, or something very specific such as helping in sports training. Take advantage of the sheer range of options.

These are not just 'for show' activities which you can simply put down on your UCAS form. They will actually give you an insight into the challenges ahead and your ability to cope with such changes. They can give you added confidence in the interview setting when answering questions such as 'How do you think you will cope with studying in a foreign environment?'

For those of you who do not have the opportunity to travel overseas as part of your preparation, there are several local options which you can consider:

English tutoring to local students. This is a potentially excellent option for several reasons. First, it demonstrates that you can cope with a position of responsibility and trust. Second, it shows your enthusiasm and ability for the English language and forces you to think about the technical grammatical issues; this will not come about simply by casual English-language conversation with peers. Third, it shows your ability to cope with yet another demand on your busy schedule, and is an extracurricular activity with an academic leaning. Last, it can be a lucrative option for you, particularly helpful if you are, for example, planning a gap year abroad.

Debating/public speaking competitions. Many countries host debating competitions using English as the medium. These can vary from school-level model UN debates to local, regional and national open competitions. Search for the options which are available, and at the very least attend an event to see the standard of competition and some of the rhetorical devices and linguistic flourishes which top students and speakers are using. If you wish to participate, all the better for you: it places you in a challenging situation that is not unlike an interview and this could be the first step on the road to a better Oxbridge applications performance.

Army cadet/junior training programme. In countries with compulsory national service, you may be required to complete a significant period of training with the army, navy or air force. Students to whom I have spoken who have done this find spending some time away from the home in an army barracks, meeting new people, learning new skills and fulfilling their duties a useful window into the future for their studies abroad. Even if there is not a national service requirement, applying to do a cadetship with a volunteer wing of the military such as the country's national guard (or, as we have here in the UK, the Territorial Army) may allow you to do some part-time training where you stay away from home. This will be invaluable for your own learning as well as the personal statement. However, do be cautious: such activities are not to everyone's taste or interest; do not simply sign up to find extra things to write on your form. It is worth considering each of your local and international options for demonstrating independence and weighing up which are the most suitable for you.

Additional personal statement advice

Building on the advice above, how can you incorporate examples of your independence and suitability to study overseas into a crowded Oxbridge-oriented personal statement? Consider these examples:

1 In my time undertaking national service with the Singapore Army, I was thrust into a new environment, strange accommodation and many new things to learn. I like to think that I thrive on challenges, and I made friends from new acquaintances whose support helped me to get through. I went on to be promoted to Second Lieutenant for my teamwork and leadership in field exercises and I feel that this experience has helped my personal development, whilst leaving me eager for my next trial in a more academic setting.

2 Through my work as a volunteer at Help Age Sri Lanka, travelling to remote parts of the country in a mobile medical unit, I worked in a team under challenging physical and psychological conditions to deliver food and educational materials to make simple differences to disadvantaged elderly people. I enjoyed learning to cope with unsettled, unfamiliar settings and challenges by sharing and reflecting with others, as well as immersing myself in the culture. I look forward to bringing the individual and social coping mechanisms from this experience to my studies in a foreign country.

It can be helpful to showcase your achievements and experiences away from your comfort zone, and demonstrate both that you have learned from them and also that you are eager for more.

Summary

- Competition is especially keen amongst international students; ensure that your academic scores are as high as possible.

- Alumni and fellow countrymen are an absolutely vital resource who may be able to help in a number of valuable ways.

- Research your contacts, and be considerate of their time.

- There may be many options from both the private and public sectors for fees assistance.

- Demonstrating independence will help convince admissions tutors that you can cope with high academic demands in a foreign setting. There are many fruitful and enjoyable methods to do this; plan ahead to make best use of your time!

Oxbridge timeline: Oxbridge application one-year plan

January	Start to plan your summer activities for this year. In order to do this effectively, undertake the following four steps: 1. You must draft a personal statement or CV listing what you have achieved so far. 2. For additional ideas, consult the extracurricular activities map (ECAM) in Chapter 5. 3. Look for what you might be missing, or what you need to build on. 4. Come up with ideas for summer.
February	Deal with the logistics of summer planning. Look into college research. Use the college selector algorithms to begin narrowing down your shortlist.
March	Use your college shortlist to investigate further details.
April	Attend open days. Use the advice in Chapter 3 to plan ahead, and make the maximum use of your time in Oxford and/or Cambridge.
May	Stop main application efforts and concentrate solely on excellent performance in public examinations.
June	Examinations: Take at least one week off after your examinations – you will need to as you would have worked extremely hard for these if you are a serious Oxbridge candidate.

July and August	This is not a summer holiday. You should be undertaking the following pursuits: 1. Work on your personal statement. 2. Aim to undertake a small amount of academic work, reading or other academic pursuit on a daily basis. Remember to keep a file of your endeavours, including brief summaries *and a line or two on personal reflection.* 3. Work experience, courses or charity work: make sure you have something which you enjoy, you are proud of and that demonstrates your ability to cope with work and hobbies with ease.
September	Application mode. Keep a diary on your wall and prepare for the next deadlines well in advance. *30 September* is the Dr See deadline for Oxbridge submission. This means your application should be complete and have received feedback from at least two sources. You will then have two weeks to slowly and carefully work on the language and finer structural points. You *must not* under any circumstances be in a situation where your teachers are giving you feedback the night before the submission deadline. This will be of poor quality and not give you time to digest the information to make best use of it. Give your teachers plenty of time and they will give you plenty of attention.
October	15 October is the usual deadline for admission. All readers of this book will have their personal statement ready, reviewed and fine-tuned well prior to this date. The Cambridge Supplementary Application Questionnaire will also be due in October, usually by the 31st of the month. Refer to Chapter 9 for further details.
November	Aptitude tests. Make sure you practise the format, and remember to discuss with your teachers for homework extensions in the weeks running up to the examinations.
December	Interviews. Refer to Chapter 11 for details of the logistics which you must undertake to prepare for your interview day itself, in addition to the academic preparation.
January	Results and pooling – time to steel your nerves!
March	Revision for summer examinations – you must ensure you get your required grades, including your A*s!
June	A2 level (or other school exit examinations).
October	The start of university life: your introduction to your college, the joys of Fresher's Week and the beginning of your academic and social journey in Oxbridge.